INSIDE PARKHURST

The Final Stretch

David Berridge

SEVEN DIALS

First published in Great Britain in 2023 by Seven Dials,
an imprint of The Orion Publishing Group Ltd
Carmelite House, 50 Victoria Embankment
London EC4Y ODZ

An Hachette UK Company

1 3 5 7 9 10 8 6 4 2

A CIP catalogue record for this book is
available from the British Library.

ISBN (Mass Market Paperback) 978 1 3996 0968 5
ISBN (eBook) 978 1 3996 0969 2
ISBN (Audio) 978 1 3996 0970 8

Typeset by BORN Group
Printed and bound in Great Britain by Clays Ltd, Elcograf S.p.A.

MIX
Paper from
responsible sources
FSC
www.fsc.org   FSC® C104740

www.orionbooks.co.uk

CONTENTS

V

PREFACE

Names and details have been changed to protect the innocent and the not-quite-so innocent (as well as the incompetent), but my experiences are an entirely representative portrayal of my time working as a very ordinary prison officer serving at HMP Parkhurst and HMP Albany, two prisons that were physically close to each other but couldn't have been more different.

As in my previous book, the stories I am telling are all taken from the time that I was in the prison service, from 1992 to 2019, and many of the terms, job titles and practices have changed since then. The language and terminology used throughout is my own and reflective of my time as a prison officer.

INTRODUCTION

Life Sentences

Claret. Everywhere. The stench was what hit you first, filling your nostrils like a butcher's shop. The walls, ceiling and window were covered in it. Bloody smears around the emergency bell showed the inmate's frantic desperation as he'd tried to summon help, the claustrophobic concrete box now more slaughterhouse than cell.

We had entered with the extreme caution of anyone entering somewhere almost entirely covered in blood. No time for protective gear. I could feel my pulse pounding with adrenaline.

The inmate slumped in the corner was losing blood at an alarming rate, his face pale and his eyes wide with fear, seemingly pleading for help. The unfortunate thing was that the only help available to him was from us, the very people he hated, those 'fucking screws'. The self-same screws who were now battling hard to save his life. A violent, cold-blooded murderer, a wretched recidivist in and out of prison his entire adult life, he'd been threatening to send a screw to hospital or the cemetery for days. However, he clearly hated himself even more. He'd cut his throat, forearms and femoral artery with an improvised home-made knife and was now in a bad way. Our hands became sticky with dark blood as we staunched, stemmed and pressed anything and everything in a desperate battle to save him. Fortunately for us – and him – the medics finally arrived and took over, eventually blue-lighting him out.

I had been on duty for less than two hours at HMP Parkhurst, home to some of the country's most notorious criminals, not even a week into my career as a screw and I was sat trying to work out what the hell had just happened. I remember being worried because I had only been issued with three white uniform shirts and now one of them was very unlikely to ever be white again. It was a little after 9.30 a.m. and my shift didn't finish until 5.30 p.m. I was already knackered. That morning, I'd already dealt with a minor head injury, done a roll check, unlocked the wing, served 135 inmates their breakfast and been covered in an inmate's blood.

The wing's senior officer (SO), a hugely experienced, short-arsed, chain-smoking Welshman, approached me as I leant against the wall of the wing office.

'Well done, Nipper. You all right – because it seems you did all right?'

I nodded vaguely.

'Then get yourself washed up, grab a quick brew and nip down the stores for a clean shirt.'

He patted me once on the shoulder and then strode off down the corridor, patting his top pocket and reaching for his cigarettes.

I was just relieved that I hadn't fucked up, hadn't frozen or let a prisoner die, but more than anything else, I was bloody relieved that I would be back to having three white shirts.

Prisons. Those ugly, slightly secretive places. Everyone thinks they know a bit about prison, though most people haven't set foot in one. There's plenty of television and films but they never seem to get it quite right. They can't show the reality of an inmate carving great chunks of flesh out of himself, or the inmate covered in shit or blood or semen, or the inmate banging his head against the cell wall as he threatens to cut his own throat. They can't show you the prison officer talking to an inmate for an hour and a half to try and calm him down. They aren't there to see the officer administer first aid to the drug addict who has cut himself so many times everyone has lost count. They can't tell you how it feels to find yet another inmate hanging. Television can't get across the stench, of sweat and cleaning products, tobacco and fear. It can't get across the noise, so loud you almost feel it more than you hear it. Most so-called normal people know just one thing about prison: they really don't want to go there.

For almost thirty years it was my daily life. To go behind the big walls. To go where we put the nasty people whom we don't want to mix with the nice people. To go where we shut away society's dirty little secrets. The drugs, the mental health issues, the suicide and self-harm. When people find out that you work in a prison (after they ask if you've ever met a famous criminal) they always ask the same question: 'What's it really like?' Somehow everyone knows that behind those impenetrable walls, it's more than the inmates that aren't ever getting out. It's the secrets.

Prisons are full of just about every extreme of human behaviour. Horrific violence, cruelty, the human flotsam of wasted lives and as close to evil as I can believe exists, but there is also kindness and compassion, heroism and selflessness as well as those secrets. They stay behind the walls, locked up tight. Prisons are secret societies and they don't welcome outsiders and intruders. It's something that the public would really prefer not to acknowledge too: out of sight, out of mind.

The actual day-to-day work of a prison officer is to be a paramedic and a psychologist, a policeman and a spy, a diplomat and a bouncer, to fight fires, literal and metaphorical, whilst trying to remain calm and non-judgemental when dealing with those deemed fundamentally unfit to inhabit society. You must, in the blink of an eye, be able to move from role to role, from serving breakfast to emergency medicine, from being a sympathetic ear to a firm hand, all with the background thrum of extreme violence never far away. You keep an eye on colleagues, you count inmates, you listen to conversations, try to read body language, aim to head off a situation before it gets serious but always be ready to jump in if it does. It's called 'jail craft' and you can't learn it from a book. When I joined HMP Parkhurst, it was full of experience and knowledge, which has now been almost entirely lost over the last two or three decades, as falling wages and difficult working conditions have hollowed out the service of senior experienced staff.

If you believe the papers, you'd read again and again that prison officers are bent, corrupt and greedy, willing to strike at the drop of a hat for *even* more money. But prison reporting has little insight into what actually goes on in the 117 prisons in the UK. Whether through ignorance or malice, from job titles that haven't been used for a generation to wilfully one-sided reporting, the result is a fundamental misrepresentation of what's going on inside.

Most people don't think about the prison service until something goes terribly wrong. The escapes. The riots. The staff member who has an affair with an inmate or gets caught bringing drugs in.

I want to bring something *out* of prison that's far more dangerous: the truth.

My previous book was an exploration of my time as a prison officer but in the process of writing it, I realised there was a different, darker book that needed to be written: the stories that I tried not to think about but always did. It's only now, with enough time and distance, that I can tell those stories. Historians think that prison officers are called screws because of the mechanism that used to lock prisoners' shackles. This book is my attempt to unscrew the locks on the things I've seen and let the truth be free.

Because it changes you, spending so much time in prisons. You can take the man out of the prison but not the prison out of the man. Twenty-eight years . . . you often get less for murder. Though I could always physically leave at the end of each shift, I saw things that will always stay with me.

It changes your understanding of what people are capable of. When you spend your life in that sort of extreme environment, it resets your sense of what 'normal' is. Over the years I encountered notorious serial killers, murderers and terrorists, as well as countless common or garden armed robbers, rapists and murderers. I spent a large proportion of my life surrounded by some of the most dangerous people in the country.

A prison officer's normal day is most people's worst day at work ever.[1] And believe me when I say that a prison officer's bad day doesn't bear thinking about. The high number of prison officers who struggle with stress, depression and

---

[1] Find me another job where having shit thrown at you is so normal, it has a slang name ('potting').

PTSD (post-traumatic stress disorder) is testament to that and academic researchers found in 2020 that the work of prison officers was 'intrinsically stressful and emotionally demanding'.[2] But I can say that, at least to begin with, I enjoyed the challenge. It was such a high-pressure environment and there was a real camaraderie, once you'd earned the respect of your colleagues. You relied on each other to remain safe in a genuinely dangerous environment. In that sort of extremity, you learn a lot about people. All the layers you find in polite society are stripped away; there's nowhere to hide.

And now, if you dare, I want to take you there.

I have never been one to sensationalise. I'm not especially brave or clever. I'm just an ordinary bloke who believes in doing the right thing when the right thing needs to be done.

Above all, I believe we should abide by the rules of a courtroom: to tell the truth, the whole truth and nothing but the truth.

---

2 Clements AJ, Kinman G, Hart J (2020) 'Stress and wellbeing in prison officers', in Burke R, Pignata S (ed(s).). Handbook of Research on Stress and Well-being in the Public Sector, edn,: Edward Elgar Publishing Ltd.

CHAPTER I

Two Juggings and a Funeral

The scream, more animal than human, made me jump to my feet and start into a run. Normally I'd hang back a bit, try to avoid the paperwork, but that cry, high-pitched and desperate, was impossible to ignore. The general alarm had been raised and we arrived at the TV room just after another officer I didn't know but who looked every inch a NEPO.[1] There, we found a panicking prisoner and the obvious source of the scream, slumped in a chair in a pool of steaming something, hands held to his face, whimpering. As we knelt down to look at him I could see the skin on one side of his now seemingly melted face, an unnatural bright pink and already beginning to drip and peel. An empty discarded jug was dropped next to him.

'Shit! We need Healthcare.' Nothing like stating the bleedin' obvious in an emergency situation!

The room was filled with the sickly smell of sugar and hot oil.

'They've used fat.'

Often when someone is 'jugged', it's with a mixture of boiling water and sugar – what the press call 'prison napalm'. The molten sugar sticks to the skin and keeps burning. The fact that the assailant (or assailants) used oil meant that cold water wouldn't even help. We radioed

---

1 New Entrant Prison Officer (prounounced 'Nee-po').

7

the hospital staff and sat next to the inmate, trying not to look at his now-disintegrating face as he shivered, moaning, until they got him off the wing.

One of the older officers came over and could see his younger colleague was shaken up.

'You all right there?' he asked.

'Yeah,' said the youngster, keen to show what he was made of. 'It's just . . . Well . . . I've never seen anything like that.'

The older officer nodded.

'Right,' he sniffed. 'I'll go and put the kettle on.'

To be in a prison like Parkhurst was to be surrounded by people whose relationship with violence is very different to most of us. Giving it, receiving it, using it. Some of the prisoners had jugged the inmate in the TV room because they found out he was inside for a particularly horrific rape. Sex offenders don't normally mix with the other prisoners but he'd run out of options everywhere else he'd been so they sent him on the wing and he'd tried to keep his head down. But some other inmates became suspicious and got someone to do some digging. It was a contract. Who knows who and who knows why? Who knows how they paid for it, or whether it was a freebie, for fun or for reputation? In the tangle of debt, favours, obligations and deals it was impossible to say. By the rules of prison, though, it wasn't out of the ordinary, or unreasonable: it was just what happened. Beatings are regularly doled out for any number of reasons, along with stabbings and maimings. I once knew a prisoner – Fred – who stabbed another inmate sixty-three times because he owed him half an ounce of baccy.[2] Fred

---

2 For the metric-minded, that works out at about five stabs a gram.

came across as a jolly, happy chap, always smiling. At first I thought he was exaggerating, trying to intimidate me, but I checked out his story and it was true.

I wasn't long into the job when Fred came to see me in the cleaning office. Once he'd gone, I noticed a couple of marker pens were missing. I found myself in a bit of a dilemma, what with Fred's penchant for extreme violence. Did I confront him about it and risk a very possibly violent confrontation, or take the sensible option and pretend I hadn't noticed? Reasoning that this was likely to be some sort of test and, having never been particularly sensible, I approached him and asked ever so diplomatically, 'Fred, I seem to have mislaid a couple of highlighter pens. You didn't pick them up by accident, did you?' Then I met his interesting gaze as he stared at me coolly. I braced myself for a degree of righteous indignation, even anger, but he just gave a friendly smile and gestured towards his cell.

'Well, I promise you, Guv, you won't find them in there or on me.'

Reasoning that there were fewer things easier to hide internally than a pen, I smiled back at him, holding his gaze.

'Well, I had to ask. I'm sure they'll turn up.'

He just nodded.

Two reasonable men talking. But amazingly turn up they did, a few shifts later. I like to think I passed the Fred test.

There's nothing that prisoners can't turn into a weapon. The classic prison shiv of a razor blade melted on to a toothbrush. Pens, pencils, rolled-up magazines, broken pool cues, sharpened plastic packaging, mop handles, even a sharpened bog brush can make a mess of someone. A common punishment or warning is to 'stripe' someone with several deep cuts on the buttocks, which has the dual benefit of being almost certainly non-lethal and making life extremely unpleasant for the recipient.

Anything heavy can be placed in a pillowcase or sock and swung at someone – a tin of beans or tuna, for example, or a couple of pool balls. When I first arrived on the wing, it was the ever-popular, ever-ready PP9 radio battery – the phrase often used in these assaults was to be 'PP9'd'. Placed in a sock or pillowcase and swung at someone, this chunky battery would, in the right hands, inflict horrific disfiguring injuries. I knew of an officer who had been first on the scene of a PP9 beating in a recess. Little more than a bloodied, pulped mess, the inmate was just about clinging on to life when he found him. The officer spewed his guts up. He was a tough, hugely experienced officer, who had been in the army and completed tours of Northern Ireland. The bloodied mess in the recess reminded him of a bomb-blast victim. But if it comes down to it, prisoners don't need anything beyond their bare hands to hurt each other.

You become used to it, or you find a new job. I didn't talk to anyone outside of work about the things I saw, certainly not my wife. I never even told anyone outside I was a prison officer; I was a civil servant as far as everyone was concerned. In many ways, I was just following the most important rule in prison – don't grass. Whatever else was going on, whatever complicated sequence of events saw you getting a kicking from someone or being stabbed in the arse, you just don't talk about it.

On my first week I was on the twos landing, talking to a more experienced officer when suddenly we were interrupted by a bit of a kerfuffle on the landing below. We looked down and realised that there was a fight and whoever was involved was doing it in the rather confined space of the small laundry room – basically a converted cell made even smaller by the two washing machines and two tumble dryers inside. Fortunately, as we got there, the two combatants immediately stopped, both covered in an assortment of scratches, rapidly forming nasty-looking welts, cuts and grazes. One had his now-shredded vest hanging off by just the one shoulder strap, the other one's bottom lip was split and his teeth were stained a uniform red. When we asked what was going on, it turned out we had rather foolishly and in our haste reached our own conclusion and of course, it was the wrong conclusion: there was no fight, both had slipped and somehow fallen to the floor, hence the injuries.

After separating them, we asked again if there was anything they wanted to talk about but they assured us everything was fine. In fact, they were friends, perfectly all right and in no need of medical attention. We were just relieved that a shedload of paperwork had been avoided but we let the other staff know that they may have been at it (just in case) with a quick note in the 'obs' (wing observation) book. Whoever built those Victorian prisons must have used some very strange building materials because I've lost count of the number of black eyes, broken noses, fingers and arms caused by walking into doors or falling down the stairs. Sometimes they were even capable of causing multiple stab wounds!

Over the years I have thought a lot about why it's such a key aspect of prison life and I think it must be that when you're in such a hostile environment, having one thing you're all on the same side about must be incredibly important to an inmate. You might be away from your family and your mates, you might be tangled up in this complicated world of debt and revenge, an armed robber battering a murderer over a drug deal someone else did to repay a third-hand debt somehow passed on to you, but at least you're not a fucking screw!

What happened in prison stayed in prison. Its own rules, its own traditions. And Parkhurst felt even more cut off than most prisons, being on the Isle of Wight. Originally a military hospital and then a children's asylum, by 1838 it was a prison for children. In the 1860s it became a prison for young male offenders and was famous, or rather infamous, for its harsh regime, including the use of leg irons. In 1968 it had become one of the first prisons in the country to have an SSU (special secure unit), where maximum-security prisoners could be housed.[3] By the time I joined, they were gutting two of the wings, fitting toilets, sprinklers and tannoy systems and replacing the old wooden floors and cell doors to try and drag it out of the Victorian age, but it was still a dark, shabby, gloomy place.

It even had its own language. One morning early on, it was my job to give the 'last call' to let the inmates know breakfast was almost finished serving (at the weekend, breakfast started at 8 a.m. and went on to 8.30 a.m.). As soon as we unlocked our landings it was always a case of give it a few minutes, watch and wait – who's woken up on the wrong side of the bed, spent the night stewing over some minor infraction, real or imagined, it didn't matter. Then, once the cleaning officer had returned from the kitchen after collecting the morning's breakfast trolley, the call would come: 'Staff to hotplate'. This was always an interesting time, because most prisoners, it would be fair to say, are not morning people – not at their best in the morning,

3 Special Secure Unit. Basically, an extra-secure prison within the prison – it was present from 1968–95.

grumpy and often hostile, even more so than normal. As I soon found out, mornings were the worst – the most volatile times, with pushing and shoving to use the recess.[4]

So there I was standing on the ones (ground floor), 'Last call, breakfast hotplate closing!' This was immediately met with a chorus of 'fuck offs', 'hold the gate, Guv', 'you're having a giraffe' and one particularly not-so-early bird still eager for his worm came down ranting and raving, saying, 'Fuck this! I haven't had my fucking acker, I'm entitled to my fucking acker and I wants my fucking acker!' I watched, mystified, as he reached the hotplate orderly – a fellow inmate, whom any sensible prisoner wouldn't want to annoy. Who very politely told him he was too fucking late for his acker and that he should fuck off back to his peter.

These peculiar terms – 'giraffe' and 'acker' – were commonly used in Parkhurst, a language derived mainly from Cockney rhyming slang. 'Acker Bilk' – milk, 'giraffe' – laugh. It was, however, a language it would take me time to master. This language was important because if an inmate approached me and said, 'I was reading the currant when I saw a tea leaf, half-inching some tomfoolery from a peter, he legged it up the apples and his Barnet was brown and he had no Hampsteads,' I was going to have to work out what he meant.[5]

---

4 Before 1993, when a law was passed that all prison cells were to have internal sanitation, this included emptying the slop buckets, the improvised toilets that used to be in Parkhurst and other Victorian prisons around the country.

5 Loosely translated, this means 'Goodness, officer, there I was reading the *Sun* newspaper, when I saw a thief pinching some jewellery from a cell before running upstairs. He was a brown-haired gentleman with no teeth.'

Mealtimes were often the location for flashpoints. One lunchtime, it kicked off big time. The hotplate was upended, hot food thrown over inmates, officers and the ceiling. Two large containers, one containing gravy and the other custard, were unceremoniously picked up and thrown at no one in particular but left the floor as slick as an ice rink. A pitched battle ensued, pushing and shoving, loud incoherent verbal threats were being thrown around as much as any of the food. Pandemonium. The whole fucking place had been pebble-dashed – the walls would probably have won the Turner Prize. In among it all, inmates and officers were slipping and rolling about. Fortunately, someone on the landing above had seen the chaos below and hit the alarm bell. The hotplate was eventually cleared and the wing banged up – not a particularly easy task because the 'mini riot' had ensued as the meals were being unloaded from the trolley, meaning that nobody had been fed and any food that had arrived on the wing to feed the wing was now, actually, part of the wing. So the chaos continued, with inmates saying in no uncertain terms that they wanted their dinner, they were fucking entitled to their dinner, they knew their rights – 'It's against our human rights! If we don't get our dinner, you'd better not unlock the wing or there will be fucking trouble . . .' Blahdy bloody blah. It was only the fact that the governor had been informed and had given the now pissed-off kitchen staff instructions to do what they do best: feed the wing.[6]

---

6 The kitchen never really cook, they just warm stuff up, or at least, that's the general opinion, but at least they had apparently done a food-warming course.

With assurances made to the now pumped-up, irate inmates, they were finally put behind their doors. The kitchen staff rose to the challenge and within forty-five minutes, with help from staff from the other wings (who couldn't leave until the prison roll was correct), we were doing a 'controlled unlock' (basically only letting out six or so inmates at a time, one in and one out) and feeding 90 per cent of the wing with eggs, chips and beans, all warmed to perfection.

In the debrief afterwards it transpired that when unloading the meals, the kitchen staff had, as always, marked the trays to indicate the contents of each particular tray. However, the tray containing 'ratatouille' had been abbreviated and simply said 'rats' (only because it was easier to spell). One of the East European inmates went mental and though not speaking much English, told every fucker that we were making them eat rats! To be fair, there were enough of the vile vermin around the prison. So they put two and two together and came up with a riot.

Prison had rules, but they were often difficult to understand.

Kettle number two

A few years into the job I was filling in paperwork in the office, having just searched a cell with another officer called Steve, when we heard the very definite sound of running. Now, the sound of running on a wing is never ever a good thing, so we immediately stopped what we were doing and reluctantly popped our heads out to try and see what was happening, ('reluctantly' because no one wants to stop doing their paperwork, as it often leads to even more paperwork). The commotion was from the landing above, where one of the inmates was in obvious distress, groping his way along the landing like a blind man, screeching and screaming. As we raced up the stairs, two officers from the landings above were coming down, hitting the alarm bell on their way. Once we all reached the inmate, it was obvious what had happened: I could now recognise that high-pitched keening, more like a baby crying or an animal in a snare than a grown man.

I checked the jug – no oil – so we shoved him in the landing showers and turned on the cold water, the troops arrived and the 'banging up' followed. Steve, my cell-searching colleague, asked the other two officers who had descended from the landing above what had happened. They said that another inmate had just walked up to the victim and thrown the boiling water over him. Never actually said a word, just walked up and threw the water, looked at him for a bit, then walked away. The inmate who carried out this 'jugging' didn't have a lot going for him – he was insular, a bit of a loner and definitely not the sharpest tool in the box. Also, short, fat and ginger. When he spoke, it was usually a long, drawn-out, slightly slurred stream of incoherent gobbledygook with a strong Mancunian accent. I don't think I ever heard him get to the end of a sentence before veering off on a tangent. The good thing about him though was that he was too thick to lie, so when asked why he had done it, he simply said, 'I only did it to protect him.' Apparently there had been a contract put out to PP9 the victim (*see also* page 10). By his own twisted logic, if he 'jugged' him, he would have to go to hospital and then he wouldn't be PP9'd. He backed up this defence by pointing out that 'it was only water'. Strangely we all found ourselves nodding, agreeing with this twisted logic.

Only in prison would the fact that it was *only* boiling water you threw in someone's face be an act of compassion.

Kicking off

Violence wasn't just the inmates though. Being a prison officer meant existing in an atmosphere saturated in violence. Disagreements between prisoners and 'kangas' often met with a stream of promises of what horribly unpleasant things were going to be done to you, your wife and kids, your dog and/or Great-Aunt Susan. Usually this was nothing more than verbal bravado, a performance put on for their peers and a bit of face saving. More often than not, once they were away from the wing, their whole demeanour would change and with no audience to play for, they would often become a little more subdued, occasionally even apologise. But things were always threatening to spill over into real violence and when they did, there was always someone looking to have a crack at an officer.

I still remember the first time it all kicked off around me. I was only a few days into the job at Parkhurst when the alert went on the radios: 'All available staff urgent assistance required. Delta wing!'[7] Me, being a keen-to-impress NEPO

---

7 Whenever there is an alarm bell situation the control room operator always uses the phonetic letter. For example, Alpha, Bravo, Charlie, Delta, etc. to give the incident location. This is done because in a noisy environment, B and D and C and E are easy to mix up. It's the same with numbers: you never say 'I'm moving with fourteen' because it sounds like forty so you always say 'one four'.

and eager to show off my impressive running speed, shot off like an Exocet missile.[8]

Sprinting across the compound, I passed half a dozen of the longer-serving officers, up multiple flights of stairs. When I reached the wing, I flew on to it, heart racing and sweat pouring, breathing out of my arse – quite literally fit for fuck all! The other, more seasoned officers were just seconds behind, fresh and ready to deal with whatever it was. Yet another lesson learned: don't be a prat, pace yourself and save enough energy to at least be productive and able to contribute something useful on arrival. After all, I could have had another four or five flights of stairs to climb before having to physically restrain a combative inmate.

Once on D wing, there was a scene of absolute chaos. One inmate was wandering about, his arm caked in blood. The wing office had been trashed with one desk turned over. Threats of violence were being thrown around like confetti, and inmates on all the landings were pushing and shoving for a better view of whatever was happening on the ones. Some inmates were descending the stairs while others were leaning over the landing railings; some seemed to be studying, counting, weighing up the odds. My mind raced. Were they tooled up? Was this planned? What the fuck had started it? Questions that for now would have to remain unanswered. For now, we had a job to do, to 'bang up' the wing. This was not going to be easy. As I stood, frozen, not sure where to start, one of the older, longer-serving officers took pity on me.

---

8   Though no officer is ever supposed to 'officially' run to an alarm bell, we always did as a colleague or indeed a prisoner might be in danger and one day it could be you that needs urgent help.

'Just get away whatever you can, no need to push it.'

I nodded, grateful. Another lesson: always stick with a seasoned pro when the shit hits the fan.

He explained when it's like this, a lot of inmates will want fuck all to do with it and just want to be behind their door. However, they can't just go behind their door, they have to be seen to be 'put' behind it. They can't be seen to be on our side and co-operating. The reason you don't push it or force it is because there will always be a couple of idiots or arseholes spoiling for a fight and an officer using force is the only excuse they need to put on a show and then it will be a domino effect, with others joining in, reluctantly or willingly. Either way, it could – and often did – escalate. It was like the bomb disposal squad: one false move, a lack of concentration, one silly mistake and the whole lot could blow up and explode in our faces.

Somewhat tentatively, I then started walking along the twos landing, trying to look confident and not frightened or fazed, while at the same time, keeping an eye out for any trouble, keeping an eye on my colleague and getting the obviously pumped-up, adrenaline-fuelled inmates back into their cells. Multitasking on an epic level, I was trying to look cool when I was actually shitting myself, trying to look as if I knew what I was doing when I hadn't a clue, trying to be a diplomat amid utter chaos. Luckily there were white shirts[9] everywhere and on my landing, five or six experienced officers, who encouraged and cajoled several inmates away.

These situations, I soon realised, required what would best be described as 'an iron fist in a velvet glove' approach,

---

9 Prison officers.

a skill I would need to learn. It was always a balancing act and this balancing act was always on the finest of lines. Caution and courage with a large dollop of tactful diplomacy were needed during those incidents and as I watched the old hands control a wing, it was truly impressive, a skill that I hoped one day to be able to put into practice. It was an invaluable skill that wasn't taught at the prison service training college because it couldn't be taught, only learned. Studying my colleagues while trying not to fuck up, I realised how professional they were. They never flapped or panicked, always remained calm and always appeared fearless, but these officers were tough.[10] As I watched them moving the inmates back to their cells, calmly and firmly but with an unmistakable air of 'don't fuck with me', I knew how much experience had gone into something that seemed so natural.

After what seemed an age, most of the wing was eventually banged up. Two inmates were removed to the Seg (segregation) unit – they walked, rather than be forcefully removed under restraint, though handcuffs were applied to both, as was normal practice. Meanwhile, they were still threatening to do all sorts of things to us.

I breathed out with relief and not for the first time over those initial weeks, thought about how I'd ended up in one of the most notorious prisons in the UK.

---

10 I had actually realised this fact soon after arriving on the wing when I had to use the gents'. The Izal toilet paper was for hard bastards only, a real man's toilet paper, none of the super-soft, quilted toilet tissue for prison officers. Oh no, Izal, with its tracing paper quality, was a character-building, arse-wiping bog roll. Anyone using Izal for such a delicate operation was tough; they had to be!

Interview

'What would you do if a prisoner has a shiv [improvised pointed or bladed weapon] to another officer's throat and is saying he'll kill him if you don't let him out of his cell?' I stared up at the two middle-aged men on the other side of the table. They were looking at me as if they were bored with life generally, but especially with me. So much for a nice gentle opener. I took a deep breath . . .

The fact was that I'd joined the prison service by accident. OK, it sounds ridiculous but it's true. I had a job at the time and although I didn't particularly like it, it was steady and paid reasonably well. My mate was unemployed and hated it, so I went along to the local job centre with him as moral support.

My mate browsed through the various job cards (remember, this was the very early nineties, almost a decade before Google and when the only book Mark Zuckerberg was interested in had talking animals in it) and he spotted one card that seemed to have potential: an advert for the job of prison officer. As I read the card over his shoulder, it sounded interesting and offered some form of long-term security with the added bonus of promotion prospects – the chance to advance in a rich, rewarding and challenging career. I told him that I'd apply as well – after all, it would be a laugh and I had fuck all to lose. I filled in the forms and a few weeks later, there was a letter inviting me to interview at HMP Shrewsbury.

It might sound bleedin' obvious, but a prison is a rather intimidating place to go for a job interview. I could never be described as one of life's natural born orators, but as we entered the gates and made our way to where the interview was to take place, I was beginning to feel properly nervous. The building was certainly doing its job of being oppressing and foreboding and making me not want to be there, and that certainly wasn't the ideal way to begin a job interview. When I was eventually called into the office, even the layout of the furniture seemed designed to put you off balance, with my chair a way back from the interviewers and so low down, I had to look up at them. The two men on the other side of the table barely acknowledged me. After they'd established it was me and I was in the right place, the older one asked me what I'd do with the prisoner and the shiv.

Shit! My mind raced as I tried to guess what they wanted me to say. Would they want someone who wouldn't freeze, who would act quickly, have their mate's back? Should I do what he wanted to keep my colleague safe, or was it like negotiating with terrorists? I could imagine that as soon as prisoners knew they could get what they wanted by threatening an officer they'd all be doing it constantly.

After a couple of seconds, the other bloke chimed in: 'He's going to kill him. You might want to speed things up, mate.'

'Well,' I said, 'do I know the prisoner?'

The first one made a face. 'What do you mean, *know* him?'

'It all depends on whether I believe he's actually going to do it. What's he in for, what's he like, what do I know about him?'

Neither of them said anything, they just made a note on the paper in front of them.

'When was the last time you were *really* angry?'

For the next twenty-odd minutes this double act fired a seemingly endless string of hypothetical questions at me, barely listening to my answers. Jumping from subject to subject, they asked me the same thing in different ways and never once gave a sense of whether I'd given the right answer or not. I was becoming dispirited and not a little bit cross as it felt like such a hostile process. Years later, I would later find out that this was the whole point: there was no right or wrong answer, it was designed to see if you panicked, crumpled or immediately lost your temper. There was no way of knowing how you'd actually act in the situations you could find yourself in, but they could definitely get a sense of whether or not you were going to be a liability.

That morning, I came out of the interview feeling like I'd been mentally mauled. I'd clearly cocked up massively and to make matters worse, I'd lost a whole day's pay and bought a train ticket for the privilege too. My wife seemed very sympathetic about the interview and understanding about the lost day's pay – a few years later she told me that she never thought I stood a chance of getting the job anyway.

I was very surprised when a few weeks after this inter-rogation, I received a letter informing me that I had been successful in my application to join the prison service (ironically, my mate hadn't been successful). Instructions were given for me to have a medical and report to HMP Shrewsbury for a two-week induction, a sort of 'try before you buy', to see if you really wanted to work inside a prison and for the prison training staff to see how you fared in such an environment.

Shrewsbury Prison was old-school. A big old Victorian jail built on the site of an even older establishment from the 1790s. As the big wooden gate slammed behind me, I could sense the history. Crowds once flocked to public executions there, and you could feel the violence seeped into the thick walls. Six of us turned up in our best suits and were issued with blue notebooks and told in no uncertain terms to stay out of the way. Each prison is a mini city, its own self-contained world, so off we went to see the gym, the library, the medical centre, the chaplain and the kitchen. As we trailed around the prison, asking stupid questions, I could tell why so many people decided it just wasn't for them – the noise, the smell, the knowledge that you were surrounded by genuinely dangerous prisoners. It was unlike anything I'd ever experienced.

I came to realise that those two weeks were really about the prison authorities observing you to see if you could hack being inside a prison, never mind being close to the prisoners. I'm six foot four, and up until that point I had always been able to back myself up physically and in most situations, but here in prison, I was constantly on edge. There was this whole world of procedure and terminology, which all of the prison officers just seemed to know and an atmosphere of everyone knowing what they were doing, while there we were, looking like work experience kids in our suits. But there was just something about it that appealed to me. There was something about the stakes involved that just felt different to the office job I was used to. In my previous role, if you made a mistake you could correct it whereas in prison someone suffered: either you, or a colleague or an inmate. Whatever your feelings on the criminal justice system, this felt like something that mattered; you were somehow contributing to something that kept people on the outside safer.

Those two weeks went by in a blur and then, before we knew it, we were training at Newbold Revel, a former country house in Warwickshire. The instructors were former prison staff of every rank. Sometimes we were sitting in a classroom at desks, much like being at school, sometimes we were role playing, some of us acting as prisoners, some acting as officers.

For nine weeks, we were taught how to do the job. We were taken through the basics of what a prison is, what it does, how to lock and unlock cell doors and search a cell. We learned first aid and health and safety, how to move prisoners and how to keep them and ourselves safe. We were taught ways of dealing with verbal conflict and (hopefully) minimising it, but we were also taught Control and Restraint (C&R), a series of grips and holds taken from martial arts which could be used to physically restrain a violent prisoner, using minimum physical force. It's a fairly safe and controlled system that allows staff to physically prevent a particular individual doing physical harm to themselves or to others, though to an outsider looking in, it looks like a mass brawl not dissimilar to any you might see outside a nightclub on a Saturday night. To see three or four prison officers remonstrating with one inmate looks horrible – three on to one always seems like an unfair fight. C&R is most definitely never intended to be a fight, but a clinical safe way of subduing a violent situation. Done well, it's clean, quick, safe and very efficient.

There were constant tests in everything we were learning, so for those nine weeks, it was eight hours a day and then homework too. After that came a passing out parade, where I somehow managed to disguise my two left feet for just long enough to complete the course.

We finished on the Friday and then started on the Monday. We each arrived at our respective prisons, where we then spent a further couple of weeks 'shadowing' officers and observed what was going on in various areas of the prison. We were taken on guided tours and given endless lists of facts and processes to memorise.[11] There was a demonstration on how to use the door jack (a heavy, cumbersome hydraulic tool for breaking down a door), a list of dos and the even bigger list of definite don'ts. Each wing we visited had a totally different feel, whether it was the noise or the smell. It was hard to put a finger on why that was but it was definitely true.

And then only a couple of weeks later, I found myself standing in the midst of a scene out of a war zone.

In the post-mortem for what had caused this particular near-riot, it transpired that it had all started during LBBs.[12] The officers had told an inmate that he would have to remove the sticks, branches and string hanging across his cell as well as dozens upon dozens of accumulated newspapers that had been used to cover the floor. He said it was to make a play area for his budgie. The trouble was that there was so much collected crap that staff had to duck and weave their way into the cell. It was a fire hazard, a health and safety nightmare and the amount of collected and accumulated crap had turned his cell into what now appeared to be a giant budgie cage. The inmate got arsey and confrontational – presumably he had particularly strong views as to the appropriate budgie habitat – and raised voices quickly escalated a once seemingly simple situation, which

---

11 Shadowing: a prison term that means 'getting in the way and annoying people'.

12 Locks, bolts and bars – a daily check by staff on the integrity of the cell to make sure that nothing has been tampered with.

had now resulted in threats being made and the near-wing riot – all because of a simple request to tidy a cell.

Over the years I found that such incidents could never ever be taken at face value. The questions would always follow. Why? Was it a cover for something else, was it designed to draw the staff into an ambush, was he in debt and needed a way to get off the wing but save face, or was he going to use the 'material' for something else – weapons, fires, etc.? Once the situation had (for now at least) been resolved, normal service could resume and once the order came over the radio net – 'Resume normal' – we all made our way back to our respective posts.

I wasn't sure if I imagined it, or if it was wishful thinking, but there seemed to be a change in my colleagues after that. It was as if I had passed some sort of test. I had realised pretty quickly that you needed to earn the respect of your colleagues and this was done by proving yourself. Not trying to be the macho hardman but simply by being reliable, trustworthy and not bottling it in a shitty situation. Only after your colleagues had decided that you were really all right and sort of reliable would they help out and offer advice: the fact that I had not yet bottled it and got stuck in was the first step.

I spent the majority of my time in the prison service at Parkhurst, which had been home to some of the most infamous prisoners in British history, including the Yorkshire Ripper, Peter Sutcliffe, Moors Murderer Ian Brady, Charles Bronson, the 'Teacup Poisoner', Graham Young, the notorious Richardson brothers, Eddie and Charlie, and of course the Kray twins, Ronnie and Reggie, along with their older brother, Charlie, Black Panther Donald Neilson, the Brink's-Mat robbers, Valerio Viccei (mastermind of the

£60m Knightsbridge Security Deposit robbery in 1987) as well as any number of terrorists, serial killers, murderers and rapists. At any point in time, the various wings, landings and especially the SSU (special secure unit) were arguably some of the most dangerous places in the country. Staff had not got the time or inclination to babysit, they needed to see if you were worth the effort or were someone who would run the other way at the first sign of trouble, cower or capitulate during confrontation, flap like fuck when not sure what to do or keep a level head. These were things that were not taught – they couldn't be – you either had the right personality or you didn't.

I also realised that you couldn't really fake it: go into a prison and try and impress, try and be something you are not would never work – it can't. In the prison environment putting on a false front and acting tough could never ever be a long-term strategy; it simply cannot be maintained. Ironically, the exact same type of behaviour pattern works for the prisoner: try and be the hardman, the alpha male type, won't work because like the officer, the inmate will eventually have to back it up. It might work short-term but eventually your bluff will be called and if you can't back up the bullshit bravado, you will get found out.

It's all about balance. You don't want someone who goes in swinging at the first sign of trouble, pouring petrol on the fire, but then again someone who doesn't get stuck in when it does properly kick off is no good either. Worse still are the ones who talk a good game but disappear at the first sign of trouble. You need to be able to trust that you have each other's back because the consequences are very real.

★

Johnson was a monster created in the gym with the help of a lot of steroids. Even I had to crane my neck up to look at him. After years of pumping iron, he was prone to paranoia, rapid mood swings and extremely aggressive behaviour. He rarely spoke and one minute he would be lying on his bed listening to music and reading, the next smashing the place up because there were two pigeons outside his cell window. This unpredictable, violently volatile inmate meant he was tricky to deal with. One day during LBBs (*see also* page 26), an officer spotted a TV aerial lead. Now this was an item that this inmate was not supposed to have in his cell. The officer asked him why he had it and informed him that he would be removing it. But Johnson was having none of it and threatened the officer with all sorts of rather unpleasant things including, memorably, the anal insertion of a fire extinguisher.

At that point, the officer made to leave the cell but was immediately trapped by the hulking presence. Fortunately, another officer outside heard the commotion and stepped into the cell just in time to see Johnson lunging towards the first officer. He grabbed the inmate's arm in what turned out to be a futile attempt to stop him. Johnson flung the officer on to the bed while at the same time shoving the other man against the wall. Another officer on the landing below heard the commotion, raced up and saw the mighty melee, raised the alarm and dived in. Now the three officers were being thrown around the cell by a pissed-off bodybuilding giant. Any hope the officers might have had of diffusing or de-escalating the situation was long gone;

Johnson was beyond reason. Even when reinforcements arrived, the carnage continued for a couple of minutes.

Fortunately, it's always a case that the big muscly types have little to no stamina – the quick, powerful aggression lasts just a short time. Once knackered and breathing out of their hoop, they are a lot easier to deal with and this was the case with Johnson. The officers were finally able to take control of him, remove him to the block (also known as the 'Seg unit', an isolation block) and the damage done could be assessed. One officer had been stabbed twice with a pen, another had a fractured scaphoid and the one who tried to confiscate the lead was so badly beaten, he never returned to work and had to be medically discharged from the prison service.

I don't want to suggest the job was all aggro – I know plenty of battle-hardened inmates who were surprised by a prison officer who gave the impression he was a cynical hardman, disciplinarian or a unsympathetic ogre, seemingly immune to the saddest sob story, who switched to a compassionate, caring professional when the situation called for it. I've lost count of the times an officer has saved the life of an inmate who has carried out the most horrendous crimes. Often someone who has been abusing them, threatening them and their families with unimaginable violence. In fact, the right use of kindness can be transformative as inmates who have spent an entire life receiving and using violence, threats and intimidation are often shocked to the core when a hard-faced screw shows an unexpected degree of compassion.

I remember hearing the story about a prison chaplain who was approached by one of the prison hardmen. Usually a nightmare, he hated the staff and any form of authority figure and was happiest when causing trouble and/or fighting. One day he received a 'Dear John' letter from his wife, telling him it was over and she wanted a divorce. Absolutely devastated and really upset, he expected no sympathy from anyone, especially his arch-enemy, the screws. He was shocked when those self-same screws were not only understanding but concerned and supportive.

On another occasion an extremely tough, screw-hating hardman was on the phone to his family on Christmas Day when his young son suddenly asked, 'Daddy, what time are you coming home?' He was so upset, he had to hang up while fighting back the tears. The staff were sympathetic and understanding and made time to talk to him and offer support. He had assumed they would take the piss and gloat, but their understanding and support had a profound effect. From that moment on, he was a changed man and his whole attitude towards his sentence and the staff changed.

However, you could never forget that in a prison like Parkhurst, we were often dealing with men for whom violence was a relatively normal part of life. Some because they simply didn't see others as people but objects and many because that's what they'd learned their whole lives from the time they were kids. Is it any wonder when you stick a load of them together in one place that becomes amplified? How else do you build or maintain a reputation but by behaving with even more extremity? In prison, the volume on everything gets turned up, and the rules on punishment and reward become more extreme. In many ways it's like a permanent war zone. What I came to realise is that violence is a tool that criminals know how to use. I had to learn to make my peace with violence, not to cause it and never to enjoy it, but not to give up control of it to them either.

But the physical restraining of an inmate is covered by a whole host of laws, conventions, rules, dos and most certainly don'ts. There is an annual Control and Restraint refresher course, once a whole day of practical exercises but now the entire morning consists of slide shows of legal points, human rights and prisoners' rights and any possible medical implications. A key principle is the officer has to use no more than 'necessary' force. The problem with this is that prisoners don't get 'bent up' on a PowerPoint slide.[13] To make a split-second judgement on how much force is necessary for a pissed-off, tooled-up, six-foot-seven-inch, screw-hating, mentally challenged, muscle-bound, adrenaline-fuelled murderer who doesn't speak English and is screaming in a language no one in the prison understands is, to say the least, a little challenging. I have been with officers who have had to restrain everyone from a dangerously deranged dwarf, a deaf inmate with learning difficulties, a one-armed inmate and another with one leg, bare-knuckle fighters and martial artists, an eighteen-stone hulk built on steroids with fuck all to lose and everything to prove, inmates as high as a kite on any number of assorted drugs or drunk on hooch, the suicidal and the desperate, naked inmates covered in blood, faeces, urine and margarine and, memorably, one inmate in a shit-covered wheelchair, brandishing an improvised blade and threatening to carve himself and anyone else who came near him to pieces.

Each and every violent episode was different and the training by its very nature cannot cater for every eventuality. At Parkhurst, incidents were regular and as part of the officers' annual refresher training, we would run through

---

13 Bent up – restrained.

recent real-life scenarios so that we could improve and adapt – basically, we would in theory learn and improve from each and every one of those incidents. Like the assortment of inmates, the location of any given incident could be equally challenging: from a barricaded, smashed-up cell to one covered in washing-up liquid, shampoo and/ or soap (fucking slippery!), shit, urine, vomit and blood. Cells littered with thousands of bits of paper and tissues ready to ignite, cells that have been flooded. Fights, threats or hostage taking could happen in places like workshops, with their vast array of potential tools, the library with a million and one possible projectiles to hand, the recess or the toilet, stairs and even the suicide netting, the exercise yard, chapel, gym, reception or the visits area full of friends and family. Similarly, a disturbance on the ones landing could set up an ambush with staff at risk from attack from above – in fact, any disturbance could be a decoy so each and every location requires a different approach and a split-second risk assessment. Officers often have to make split-second decisions while their thought processes race and decide on what to do and how to do it, what the implications are, could and should the situation escalate or could it be diffused, is there enough staff immediately to hand and if so, are they the right staff?

The problem is that C&R is, like anything, something that needs to be practised, and practised regularly. The benefits of regular use are that the officers become adept and proficient, which in turn breeds confidence. Confidence is one of those strange invisible things that can actually be seen and felt – felt by the others in the team and seen by the inmate and a lack of confidence is very often all that the inmate needs when deciding on 'fight or flight'.

Basically, without regular use and regular practice an officer becomes stale, which in turn means they become slightly less than confident and less proficient. You start second-guessing yourself. It's bad enough when you're sent in for a planned removal. As you get kitted up, pulling on your protective gear, you fumble with bits of Velcro and unco-operative buckles, your heart rate rises and you become ever so slightly uncoordinated; the helmet you've got is slightly too big, the overall too small and you're trying to tie your bootlaces with sweaty hands. You have time to wonder if you've remembered the difference between a gooseneck and a triangular fix and which direction your various rotations go. You're then given a briefing which you only half-hear, final instructions to the inmate are given only after every avenue has been explored and exhausted, the door opens and in you go.[14] You fumble about and eventually after a bit of a struggle, the inmate is both 'Controlled and Restrained'.

I personally always preferred the 'spontaneous' situations, the ones where one minute you're talking bollocks about the latest bit of scandal – who's shagging who, the latest shite decision or last night's football match – when bang, crash, wallop, there's a fight or something that requires an immediate response. The spontaneity of which causes an

---

14 Each planned 'use of force' incident is supervised and overseen by a supervising officer. This would either be a custodial manager (CM), normally O1 (radio call sign for a principal officer) or a governor, normally Victor 2 (duty governor), Healthcare would be contacted and a member of the Healthcare staff would be present to oversee and advise on any medical concerns. Once the situation is brought to a satisfactory conclusion, the hard work begins and debriefing and paperwork take place.

immediate reaction and thereby negates the problematic pondering that often goes with the planned removal.

It was never a straightforward case of opening a cell door and half a dozen hairy-arsed screws pile in to drop the twat. It's actually a well-thought-out and well-practised process, which in turn reduces the chances of anyone getting unnecessarily hurt. Each officer involved has their own specific role to play – it's not an uncontrolled free-for-all – and in my twenty-eight years I never saw uncontrolled aggression, bullying or uncalled-for violence.[15]

The world we all live in on the outside, where violence is relatively rare, is a privilege. It must be protected. Anyone who doesn't know the noise a man makes when he has boiling water thrown in his face should be grateful to those who do.

When I joined the prison service, it was staffed with experienced, capable people and part of that skill set was the ability to handle the physical side of things. By the time I left, it was mostly drained of that. Meeting violence with gentleness and understanding is a lovely idea and, who knows, maybe far cleverer people than me have worked out that it will ultimately work, but in the short term, I can't help but see it as a recipe for disaster.

Years later, a prisoner's budgie died and he held a little budgie funeral where, I am reliably informed, one of the younger prison officers cried.

---

15 At least not from officers.

CHAPTER 2

Fear on C Wing

No one knows how long Patrick Mackay sat and watched Father Anthony Crean bleed to death. He'd smashed his head in with an axe and stabbed him repeatedly in the head and throat, leaving his body in a bath full of bloody water. When the police interviewed him, he was reported to have said, 'The human body is a funny thing, the anatomy.' He subsequently confessed to thirteen murders including hurling a young girl from a train, stabbing a grandmother and her four-year-old grandson to death and drowning a tramp in the Thames, but later retracted all but four of them. At his trial, he was convicted of three counts of manslaughter (as police had been unable to identify the tramp he claimed to have killed). This was 1975; by this time, Mackay had been in and out of mental institutions, having been diagnosed as a psychopath when he was fifteen. He'd been torturing animals to death since he was ten, reportedly roasting the family tortoise alive in the back garden. He had taken to carrying around dead birds and 'fondling' them. He became obsessed with the Nazis and filled his flat with memorabilia.

By the time I met him, he'd been in prison for almost half his life after being found guilty of three of the five murders they'd eventually charged him with. He didn't speak to me, I don't think he even looked at me; he didn't speak to anyone. He had toed the line and to all intents and purposes was a model prisoner, quite withdrawn and not a discipline problem but there was something about him that made the hairs on the back of your neck rise up. He would be just sitting there and you'd get that feeling in your guts. It was something primal like a shark's mouth rising towards you out of deep water.

When you work in prison, you learn a lot about fear. The whole place stinks of it. Fear of the violence used as punishment, of being caught doing something you shouldn't be doing by the officers. Fear of catching the wrong person's eye. Underneath the anger and the aggression and the boredom: fear.

The majority of prisoners, even in somewhere as extreme as Parkhurst, weren't really predators once they were inside. Most of them were more like gazelles, timidly sniffing the air as they move back and forth from the watering hole. But in Parkhurst there were sixteen genuine fuck-off lions and those were the prisoners behind the doors in C wing. It was there that I met Patrick Mackay.

C wing was a secure special psychiatric unit. A national resource where they put the sixteen most dangerous inmates in the country. Broadmoor was a hospital for those with at least a hope of treatment. C wing in Parkhurst was where they put the people they just needed to be away from everyone else.[1] And I volunteered to be there. I did it because I wanted to test myself against the most challenging inmates there were. It involved an intense residential course and an interview.

By that point, about three years in, I felt like I had got the basics of working in Parkhurst down a bit. I had quickly realised that prison was like no other place on earth. On the

---

1 Any time you're someone 'too dangerous for Broadmoor', you have to be taken pretty seriously.

outside, a polite question such as 'excuse me what's your name?' was a simple, innocuous question. However, as I soon found out, in prison it was an opening gambit, ripe for exploitation. If an inmate realised that you did not know his name, you were fucked on so many levels. For instance, the inmate could – and often would – give a false name, almost certainly someone he hated and then that particular (falsely) named inmate could be dropped in the shit when the inmate told the officer 'go fuck yourself' because if the officer then placed the inmate on report, it would be the wrong person. That mistake could then be used to threaten that officer, or gain leverage. Or he could take the named inmate's food or give the name of a friend and those fuckers would collude, working together to exploit the situation.

One inmate might tell me his name is John Smith, so I hand over Smith's mail, food, gym slot, etc. and then the real John Smith makes an appearance, wanting to know why his private mail has been given to someone else, where's his food, he's entitled to his food and he wants his fucking food! So memorising names and faces was more than about being efficient, it was a survival skill. You had to learn the names of all the cat As (category A prisoners) and which cell they were in. On the wing I started on, that was forty. Once I was a cleaning officer, I had to learn the name of every single inmate on the wing – 135 inmates.[2]

---

2 There was a lot to keep on top of with this job as you were responsible for keeping the wing stores and laundry up to date, paying the inmates who were working as wing cleaners (and checking that they were actually doing anything), managing the process of inmates choosing their meals a week in advance and then making sure everyone got the right thing at the hotplate server area.

Another scam for the new officer who hadn't taken the time to memorise names and faces would be for an inmate to take his own cell card, place it in an empty cell cardholder and ask the officer to then unlock that particular empty cell. The unsuspecting officer might even check the card and then check and confirm the inmate's ID, but even if that matched, if he didn't know who went where and he opened the cell, the bullshitting chancer could nip in and trash the place, shit up or steal things.[3] He then comes out and replaces his cell card back into the original cardholder, while the actual cell occupier returns and finds his cell trashed, shit up or stuff missing. Someone then grasses up the officer, who obviously denies unlocking an empty cell but enters into a world of poo, made worse by three or four witnesses who confirm that the 'bullshitting chancer' never spoke to the officer and certainly never asked for the wrong cell to be opened.

I vividly remember it happening to a NEPO when I was a bit more experienced. It was one of those gorgeous, sunny, weekend days. Consequently, that morning's exercise was going to be busy and most of the wing were out on exercise.[4] Once the hour was up, it was all hands on deck, counting the inmates back and unlocking cell doors that most inmates wisely lock. I was just returning to the cleaner's office when a rather angry voice shouted, 'Who

---

3   Shit up: a classic prison punishment or warning that involves using faeces, which comes in various grades. More about this later.
4   It's those sorts of days when the NEPOs are unofficially barred from doing the exercise. They get to do the exercise when it's cold, wet, windy and miserable and over a slow, long period of time you work your way up the pecking order. Basically, NEPOs get the shit jobs and the experienced prison officers get the good jobs.

the fuck's been in my peter?!' With that, the inmate came storming down to the ones all the while shouting that some cunt's been in his peter (cell) and half-inched his snout and sugar and was now threatening to do some serious damage to whoever was responsible. This was all a little confusing if only because this con was a loner, he didn't mix and was usually quiet. Most of the wing had been on exercise and his cell door had been locked.

There were four staff on the wing and two on the landings, me in the cleaning office and the senior officer doing whatever SOs do in their office on a sunny weekend morning. It wasn't me that unlocked the cell and it wasn't the SO, so by the simple process of elimination it had to be one of the two officers on the landing, who both emphatically denied doing so. However, when questioned, it transpired that one officer had unlocked that particular cell but only for the occupier. But confusingly, it was the occupier who had been on the exercise yard and had returned to a burgled cell.

The officer who had only been in the job for a short time and normally worked in the gate had been approached by the mysterious 'occupier', who asked him if he could unlock his cell because he had left his baccy in there. The officer checked the cell card against the inmate's ID card, unlocked the cell door and then returned to the end of the landing. However, inmates being inmates, they had spotted the new face on the wing, who they quickly realised was a little less than confident and certainly not comfortable on a landing and decided it was too good an opportunity to miss. The necky cell thief simply swapped the cell card with his own, hoping the officer wouldn't check the actual number, then showed the officer his ID card matched the cell card, gained access and nicked what needed to be nicked. When the officer wasn't looking, he swapped the card back, got changed, grabbed a coffee and no doubt smoked and sold his ill-gotten gains.

There was a huge amount of essential information to absorb. Each shift started in the same way, with the SO giving a quick briefing with regards to any events, news, problems, etc. that may be relevant – i.e. the inmate in a particular cell had a 'Dear John' letter or family member had died or more commonly, we were 'lifting one' (taking an inmate to the Seg unit).[5] This was done prior to unlocking the wing because it was a lot easier to move one inmate when all the others were behind their doors. Moving one to the Seg when the whole wing was unlocked could be fraught with danger. Once any inmates had been moved, we would all make our way up on to our respective landings: two officers per landing, one on each side. We would then do a headcount of our side of the landing, total up the two sides and inform the senior officer of the landing numbers. Once all the landings had reported their numbers to the SO, they then checked that the numbers corresponded with the wing roll. If so, the SO then gives the order to 'unlock the wing'.

You always had to leave any empty unoccupied cells locked. If an inmate had been taken to Seg, or for a hospital appointment or for any other reason, their cell would have

---

5 The Segregation unit – sometimes known as 'chokey' or 'the block'. This was the punishment block where an inmate could be taken if their behaviour meant they had to be removed from their wing. It was where the most troublesome inmates on the main wings ended up and to work there, you had to volunteer specially and be approved by the other officers as they needed to be able to completely rely on every single officer there.

no cell card as these were always taken off and slid under the door. I was told in no uncertain terms that you never, ever open an empty cell unless another officer is there with you, because inmates would exploit the fact that you have been in a cell on your own and therefore could have nicked something. In fact, just in case, the inmate would often have removed an item of value – trainers, a watch, for example – and given it to his mate for safekeeping. If you went into the cell on your own then they could claim you'd broken or damaged a particular item (which, of course, had been broken for weeks) and claim for a replacement, stating only an officer could unlock a cell so it stands to reason that an officer had nicked or broken the item.

At Parkhurst, we only ever did Locks, bolts and bars (LBBs) in pairs for that reason. One officer goes into a cell, carries out the LBBs, while the other waits outside that cell, keeping an eye out before moving on to the next one when the roles are reversed. The savvy, more experienced officer knows which cells to avoid – the cell with the confrontational arsehole or the one that stinks of all things unpleasant – so they count the cells and know whether to do the first or second cell, leaving his opposite number to do the worse cell. Again, this is the sort of thing that doesn't get taught in the training college. After only a few weeks at the coalface, I realised that a lot of what we had been taught and tested on was bollocks. In the classroom it was about the rules, but in real life there was a complex set of strategies and counterstrategies between inmates and officers. Decades of wisdom passed down on either side that wasn't present anywhere in a book.

Once the landing had been unlocked, breakfast finished and the half-hour's exercise was done and dusted, it was back on to the landing for 'bang up' (locking up time). Every inmate was banged up, then staff that were detailed workshops went off to man their posts and the collator then gave each of us our 'unlock list', a list containing the names of those inmates and only those particular inmates who were to be unlocked for work. We waited on the landings while listening to our radios. Once everyone was in place and where they should be, and once the collator was happy, we were given the clear instruction to 'unlock the wing'. Once every inmate was out of their cell and the landing cleared, with the 'gate secured', basically everyone that was supposed to leave the wing had now left so we could unlock the wing cleaners and have a brew before getting stuck into the LBBs. Occasionally we would have to go and unlock an inmate later on for a Healthcare appointment, interview, etc.

You had to pay attention to everything. Very early on, I stood making polite small talk with an experienced officer, both of us looking down the landing, when he turned to me and said, 'Here we go, get ready,' and started to walk slowly down the left-hand side of the landing with me close behind. On reaching a particular cell, he told me to hit the alarm. Fortunately, it was only a couple of cells away. The noise was instantaneous, as was the reaction. Loud footsteps, jangling key chains and loud shouts of 'bang up!', all within a nanosecond of the alarm being raised.

I got back to the cell to see my colleague trying to talk to a seemingly unconscious inmate covered in claret and contorted in a most unusual way. A small smouldering pile of clothes lay on the floor. The troops arrived and not far behind, the scab lifters (medics) turned up and shortly afterwards carted him off to the hospital but not before telling Oscar 1 (O1), the principal officer in charge, that 'it wasn't serious'. The colleague I had been standing next to earlier then came out of the cell and told O1 the name of an inmate who had come out of his cell, who lived on the landing above. Staff went to his cell and swiftly removed him, taking him to the block. I had noticed fuck all but my colleague who was talking to me and asking questions had been aware of everything. Especially experienced prison officers have a skill set bordering on a sixth sense – they seem to see things without looking, hear inaudible things and interpret the slightest nuance of behaviour. You had to be aware of everything but somehow act as though you weren't, something I too learned early on.

One day I was detailed as one of the two officers at the tailor shop, where inmates could work on cutting and sewing fabrics (this particular group didn't seem to contain the most industrious of individuals though). First of all, I diligently counted the thirteen prisoners who came in, as they shouted out different random numbers to try and put me off.

Then, as tools such as scissors and knives were carefully dished out, I was hypervigilant, aware of how easily they could be used as a weapon against each other or us officers. I sat up at my little table, watching them like a hawk, as they laughed and swore at each other. After about a quarter of an hour the cleaning officer came in and dropped off two cat A books. So now I knew that two of the inmates were cat As.[6] I was getting the hang of this. Fascinated by

---

6   Cat A books were blue, passport-sized books that acted as an ongoing hourly documented record of each of the cat A prisoners' locations and movements, signed every hour to confirm that particular cat A's exact whereabouts at any given time.

the variety of shapes and sizes, accents and personalities that prison contained, I kept up my watch. Every time I glanced over to the other officer, a portly bloke in his fifties, he just seemed to be engrossed in his motorcycle magazine and not paying much attention at all. Confused by this cavalier approach to the job, I reasoned he must just be a slightly jaded, lazy twat.

Then the gate opened and the principal officer, O1, entered.[7] I sat up even straighter (if that were possible), but he walked past me and made straight for the other officer, who had somehow magically swapped his magazine for the observation book.[8] My colleague immediately informed O1 that we had a roll of 'thirteen with two' (thirteen inmates with two cat As), one was in the khazi and furthermore, the instructor had confirmed with Healthcare that inmate Thomas could wear flip-flops as the doctor had given him the OK due to his medical condition and Smithson appeared to have a new tattoo.

I was impressed on so many levels. On the surface my erstwhile colleague had appeared to not even be paying attention – I hadn't seen or heard him counting, let alone taking a note of what was going on. I, on the other hand, had been sitting there, trying to take everything in and had missed so much: the flip-flops, the new tattoo and the fact that one inmate was in the khazi. Once O1 was happy, he

---

7   Oscar 1 is the call sign for the person in charge.

8   The wing 'obs book' or observation book is a bit like a ship's logbook. It is there as a source of reference. Anyone working on a particular wing can record and make note of things that may be of interest, rumours going around, who's had a 'Dear John', etc. Staff usually grab it and have a quick read to catch up and make themselves aware of what's occurring on the wing prior to each shift.

signed the cat A books and then left. I tried to commit to memory the face of the two cat As.

Suddenly, there were just fifteen minutes to the end of this session. The instructor shouted, 'Tools in, lads,' and I looked carefully as knives and scissors were handed over and the shadow board checked and signed for. Once happy, he gave my colleague the thumbs-up. Informing the control room via the radio that we had 'tools correct' (basically all the tools had been accounted for with none missing), we waited a few minutes for the other workshops, gym, etc. to get ready and the route back to the wings to be manned, the gates opened and officers and Zulus in their respective positions along the route back to the wings to make sure the inmates stuck to the proper route and didn't wander off elsewhere.[9] When everyone was happy, the instruction was given: 'All stations, we have main movement workshops back to wings.'

We rub down searched and counted every inmate leaving, 'swept' the shop, i.e. went round and checked that everything was in order, no fires had been lit, no machines left running and all the areas such as the toilets and cupboards were clear of any inmates.[10] Once all the workshops reported that they were happy, we headed back to the wings. As we walked through the compound area, I took the opportunity to quiz my motorbike enthusiast fellow officer.

9　Zulus: dog handlers.

10　When I started working at Parkhurst, every inmate was, without fail, rub down searched prior to moving from a building, i.e. before leaving the workshops, education, the wing exercise, etc. However, during my last years in the prison service, this had become far less common – certainly in HMP Albany, where I finished my career.

'How did you know all that when you'd been reading your bike magazine the whole time?' I gasped, unable to keep the curiosity out of my voice.

He just winked at me. 'If one of them thinks you're watching and are interested, they'll fuck about and do something so you have to watch them, just so someone else can do some real shit where you're not watching. If you act like you can't be arsed or aren't watching, they'll carry on with their normal behaviour. If they're up to any shit, they're only going to be doing it where they think you're not watching. Simple.'

I thought back to me counting out loud and I realised that I was going to have to learn how to pay attention without looking like I was. Gradually, though, I got my head around what I needed to and that led me to C wing.

Always the quiet ones

The first thing that struck you on C wing was the silence. The other wings were almost permanently noisy: prisoners calling out to each other and officers, swearing, laughter (and sometimes screaming), banging and crashes. C wing was clean and quiet. It reminded me of a library. This was partly because many of the inmates were on some form of medication to try and calm them but it also felt like so much of the noise was a performance, an attempt to project bravado, to try and establish your place in the food chain. The prisoners in C wing didn't need to do that, they weren't part of the day-to-day of prison life. On a normal wing, if an inmate didn't like you, you knew it. He told you, he threatened you and he made your life unpleasant. However, with these inmates, you didn't know if they liked you or not and you got a sense that it simply didn't matter. They could quite happily put a knife in you for no particular reason other than they decided that today would be that day and you just happened to be there.

Another who I'm happy to admit scared the shit out of me was multiple killer Robert Maudsley. Too dangerous to mix with the other inmates, every single thing he did had to be with a number of staff present. He had been christened 'the real-life Hannibal Lecter' by the press. When serving time for a murder in 1977 at Broadmoor, he and an accomplice took a fellow inmate – a paedophile – hostage. Over the next nine hours he tortured him with a knife made from a sharpened plastic spoon before killing him by ramming the spoon into his ear. This was reported as 'his head cracked open like a boiled egg, with a spoon hanging out of it' and the legend that Maudsley had eaten some of his victim's brain was born. His reputation was confirmed when the following year he murdered two more inmates on the same day, hiding the first in his cell and under his bed before going on the hunt for his next victim. Once the second victim had been dispatched, Maudsley calmly walked over to an officer and informed him that during the next roll check, there would be 'two off the roll'.

In later years, the press would delight in describing the glass cage he was confined to beneath Wakefield prison as 'Monster Mansion'. It has been reported that to get to it, you have to pass through seventeen steel doors and the only furniture is a table and chair made of cardboard. A metal toilet and sink is bolted in place and Maudsley sleeps on a concrete slab with a mattress.

He was escorted everywhere with his own personal entourage and had a small exercise yard. He was alone, as he had been and probably will be throughout his remaining time inside.[11] He did, however, have a football, which was constantly and repetitively bounced against the wall – even that simple act was menacing. Friends and family have described him as kind, gentle and intelligent, he has been reported to love poetry, art and music, even has a genius-level IQ. But I can tell you, spending even five minutes near him scared the shit out of me. There are plenty of clever people who believe that locking up people and throwing away the key is morally wrong, but I for one can sleep easier at night knowing that he is never getting out.

Neil Bracey was another inmate on C wing. Bracey was from Neath in South Wales and the press had dubbed him the 'body in the boot' killer. In 1990 he was sentenced to life imprisonment for the horrific killing of his 24-year-old ex-girlfriend, Alison Farrell. He had not only bludgeoned and beaten her with a hammer, but then strangled her with rope. While she was still alive, he shoved her in the boot of his car and calmly drove over a thousand miles – even picking up a hitch-hiker along the way – while she slowly died in the boot. In 2003, Bracey was found hanged in his prison cell shortly before getting parole.

Darren Blanchflower (or 'Danny' Blanchflower as he was called on C wing) was another dangerous inmate, though at first not thought to be in the least bit dangerous or violent. He was initially serving a three-and-a-half-year sentence at HMP Norwich for robbery and it was during this time that his hitherto predilection for extreme violence first manifested itself. It was during one of the prison's painting

---

11 As I write, Robert Maudsley has been imprisoned for more than forty years.

and decorating courses that Blanchflower's poor standard of work had been rightly or wrongly criticised by a civilian instructor. Rather than disagree, argue or remonstrate, Blanchflower simply picked up a hammer and repeatedly hit the instructor about the head. The instructor was in a desperate life-or-death struggle and hearing the screams, a prison officer quickly arrived on the scene, shouting at his assailant to stop. Blanchflower then stopped, stepped back, looked at what he had done and then carried on beating the now-defenceless instructor until he was dead. Later, in interviews, Blanchflower opened up about his unhappy childhood, explaining that he used to starve his pet rabbit to see what happened and eventually killed it by cutting it in half with a spade. He then went on to explain how he used to use an old mangle that he had been given to crush small animals. He was also featured in an article in the *Daily Mirror* in which he expressed remorse for his crimes.

As you can imagine, individuals capable of such actions had to be handled incredibly carefully. Every rule that was present on the other wings was even more important here.

This became clear with Joe Purkiss, who was originally imprisoned in 1984 for attempted murder. A dangerous and problematic prisoner from day one, he had been diagnosed as having psychopathic characteristics. Previously in the Rampton Secure Hospital, he had a horrendous record. He was in C wing because nowhere else in the country could manage his disruptive behaviour. In 1996, while at Wakefield, he took a fellow inmate who was a sex offender hostage and tied him to a chair. For five hours they negotiated before Purkiss slit his throat and stabbed him in the chest three times. Previously he had said that he wanted to 'kill all nonces'.[12] The rumour was that fellow inmates had been taking bets on whether he would kill his hostage or not.

It's often hard to put a finger on what makes you feel that fear, but for some reason it was almost always the quiet ones. Often it wasn't the ones who explicitly threatened you, shouted the odds, got in your face or squared up to you. One such individual was in the Seg unit and in the back cells. Normally a classic arsehole – a violent and non-conforming destructive type – he was tall, at least six foot six, and built like the proverbial shithouse. One week, I was on nights and he was on 'thirty-minute obs', which meant I had to check on him every thirty minutes and sign the ACCT document to say I had seen him alive and well.[13] Not as easy as it might first appear because he had smeared excrement and who knows what else over his cell door's observation panel. Fortunately, the back cells had a number of discreet spyholes, one of which was set up high and required me to climb a small flight of stairs.

My first observation during the initial roll check confirmed that he was there alive and well so I signed the ACCT document to say that the inmate was seen standing in the middle of the cell with his back to the door, facing the wall. What I didn't say, because I wasn't quite sure

---

12 As an aside, years later, the serial rapist would win his case for compensation against the Home Office for failure to prevent the attack against him. He received £12,000.

13 An Assessment, Care in Custody and Teamwork document needs to be signed regularly and at given intervals to confirm an inmate judged to be a suicide risk is still alive.

how to say it, was that he slowly turned and looked – no, stared – back at me. I was pretty sure there was no way he could tell I was there. As I made my way up the staircase I was quiet – there was no noise as I gently opened the spyhole. Half an hour later, I was even quieter and watched as he stood in the exact same spot. Again, he turned to stare up at me. This happened for the next three and a half hours. I was impressed but it occurred to me that he might know that I was checking on him every half-hour so I went to look at him in between checks to see if he was taking a cheeky sit down then. He wasn't – he remained rooted to the exact same spot and again, he turned and stared. This carried on all night until I was relieved of my duties at 7 a.m. Twelve hours without moving had not only impressed me but also rattled me and every one of my twenty-five entries in his ACCT document reflects this.

To be honest, even outside of C wing and Seg, you encountered situations with the potential to shit you up. An example of this was during one of my very first nickings, where the inmate happened to be one of the big hitters on the wing, a well-known cat A.[14] Now, with me being a NEPO and not wanting to fuck up, my first nicking had to be spot on. So I wrote it out, I checked it, I corrected it and then I rewrote it. The next day, I was summoned to the Seg unit. The staff were as good as gold, ran me through what was about to happen, where I was to stand, etc. But it didn't help calm my nerves – I was shitting myself at having to present my evidence by reading it out

---

14 This is where the prisoner is written up for breaking a prison rule and the governor presides over the process for deciding what the punishment will be.

aloud in front of my fellow officers, a governor, a senior officer and, of course, the inmate himself.

The inmate was escorted in by two Seg unit officers, who stood either side and just behind him, so close that it would have been difficult to get a fag packet between them. The charges were read to him by the SO. I read my evidence: 'Sir, at the time, date and place stated . . .' etc., etc. Once this was done, the governor asked the inmate, 'How do you plead?' So I braced myself for the inevitable 'not guilty' and the verbal sparring match that was sure to follow. I sort of expected this only because he was a wily old con and I was the brand-new, shiny, untested NEPO. 'Guilty,' he admitted, 'it's fair enough, Guv – the kanga got me bang to rights.' I breathed a huge sigh of relief, one that I hoped hadn't been seen. Once the inmate had been escorted back to his cell, I left the adjudication room after having been told by one of the officers, 'As long as you never lie or try and stitch up a con, you'll always be fine.'[15]

---

15 These days it's a very, very different story. For example, that same 'nicking', for a start to place an inmate on report (the official term for nicking), is now such a complicated, convoluted and time-consuming process with any outcome so inconsequential that it's almost not worth the effort. Today's inmate wouldn't know how to plead guilty. He wouldn't see it as a 'some you win, some you lose' 'bang to rights' situation, but a personal slight. Nine times out of ten he would plead not guilty because he would feel that the officer was digging him out, the officer was a bully, the officer never liked him and he had had such an awful childhood – wasn't breast-fed as a baby and his Great-Aunt Gladys died three years before he was born, he never stood a chance . . . So in all probability it would go to an independent adjudicator, costing the taxpayer a small fortune and delaying the whole process – a process that would in all probability fully understand the unfortunate inmate's desperate plight.

Frightening the kangas for sport was a general prison pastime. One evening I was sitting in the fours observation box, watching the toing and froing of the inmates while willing my watch to reach 21.00 so that we could start 'banging up' the wing. Out of nowhere a pool ball came flying towards the obs box, hitting the perspex with an almighty crack which was amplified many times over in the small confines of the box. It made me jump and almost in need of a change of underwear. As an inmate approached, I braced myself for whatever was to follow. Clocking the alarm bell out of the corner of my eye, I was ready to quickly hit it when the inmate bent down, retrieved the pool ball and said, 'Sorry, Guv, it was an accident – I miscued.' Like him and the other inmates, I knew it was no such thing and the twats had thrown the ball to make me jump. It worked and as he walked away, they laughed. Regaining my composure, I smiled to myself more out of relief and grateful that it wasn't an attack, just their idea of high jinks.

An explosive celebration

One time, very early on, I absolutely shat myself and it was all David Platt's fault. Back then, I was overly keen, enthusiastic and on high alert. In those days, two officers worked nights on B wing. My oppo, who had been in the job for years, took a far more relaxed approach to nights, using his time far more wisely reading golfing magazines and a couple of magazines that shall we say were of a 'special interest'. He also spent time sorting out his holidays, eating junk food and cleaning the tea/staffroom while I did the majority of what was called 'pegging'. This involved going to each of the various landings, inserting a small key into a small silver plate attached to the wall and turning in a clockwise motion. This was done every half-hour to let the control room know that we were alive and well. However, the reality was to let them know we were still awake.

We hadn't been on duty long and shortly after finishing the obligatory roll check and various bit of paperwork, I had got the kettle on and was making the brews when all hell broke loose. BANG! It sounded like a bomb had exploded. This initial explosion was immediately followed by door kicking, loud shouts and cheering. With over 100 cell doors being kicked, the noise was both frightening and loud. Was it the IRA? Had they somehow managed to get the ingredients for a bomb and blown their way out? Would I return to the wing to find the inmates cheering in the smoke and rubble? I ran back to the office, only to find my oppo was sitting exactly where he had been – if anything, he looked even more relaxed by this time.

'I thought you were making the brews,' he said, puzzled, looking up from his magazines.

'What the fuck was that?!' I spluttered.

'Hmmm?' he said, looking at me curiously.

'That enormous fucking bang and the whole place losing their shit.'

He paused for a moment, as if he genuinely couldn't work out what I was talking about. Then I watched as he caught up.

'Oh, that . . . England must have scored. Milk and three sugars, please.'

It turned out that unbeknown to me, it was a group match in the European Championships and David Platt had just scored. I took a slightly closer interest in the England football fixtures from that point on, if only to avoid a heart attack.

Credible threat

As I've said, most of the time, threats from inmates were like water off a duck's back to officers. The threshold for verbal and threats of physical violence was lower than you can possibly imagine. In everyday life, someone doesn't threaten to cut your fucking head off because they've missed breakfast!

But there were exceptions.

The first time I was properly scared we were escorting the inmates to and from the wing to the library. To get there, we had to walk through a covered walkway known as 'birdcage walk'.

Two officers would collect their respective wing's inmates, collate and confirm the number of inmates, including the cat As, then ask for permission to move to the library with one officer at the front opening the gates and counting the inmates that went through while the one at the back locked gates and kept an eye out for stragglers. After arriving at the library, our roll was given to the control room, the cat A books were signed and after the allocated thirty minutes we made the return journey. That day, we only had twelve inmates but by accident or design we were moving slowly, very slowly, and as the officer in front reached the penultimate gate, he looked at me. I acknowledged him, he unlocked the gate and went through, followed by the front group of inmates.

I was at the back with an inmate who was either a raspberry[16] or an arsehole, moving irritatingly slowly. I guessed he was doing this for one of two reasons: to annoy the hell out of me or more likely, because he had been told to. This

---

16 Raspberry ripple – cripple.

was likely because this particular inmate was a member of the IRA, or at least a sympathiser. In prison, they operated like POWs, trying to work out the weak spots, memorising routines, always looking for something they could exploit. Generally, they liked to hinder the smooth running of the prison regime and would take any given opportunity to put the proverbial spanner in the works. They would, with the help of a fellow member or sympathiser, do just enough to be a pain in the arse. This was what I thought was happening now. So was this idiot deliberately going so slowly to piss me off or to separate and split the group? If so, why? Either way, I was slightly annoyed but unwilling to give the inmate the satisfaction of knowing this. Me being a clever twat decided to play him at his own game and dropped back a bit, got right behind him in his blind spot and matched his footsteps. Just as I was thinking to myself, see how he likes it, he stopped, slowly turned and looked me in the eye. As if in slow motion, he raised an arm pointed with what I noticed was a very well-manicured finger and said in his thick Northern Irish brogue, 'I'll see you on yer fucking knees!' I'm sure – or at least I hoped – he hadn't seen my involuntary buttock clench or my heart skip a beat but he might have seen me take a slight gulp. Luckily, he turned back and carried on. He wasn't loud, aggressive or particularly violent, but it was quietly deliberate, very menacing and very purposeful.

It was a good job I only ever cycled or ran to work because there's no way I would have felt safe turning the key to start a car for a very long time after that. Every single prison officer has had multiple times when it's brought home to them that what has become routine and everyday – to be around the most dangerous men in the country and be the one telling them they can't do what they want to do – has made them the target for their anger and revenge. But that's the job: you can either suck it up or find another one.

Because that's the thing about 'fear: you can't let it paralyse you. I've seen so many people freeze when it comes down to it. Thirty years working in a prison, you learn an awful lot about fear. You learn not to ignore it – there's a very good reason why you shouldn't go about petting brightly coloured snakes but equally, you can't let it rule you.

So much crime, especially terrorism, relies on fear and/or intimidation for them to get what they want. What you need to do is try and take a step backwards, assess what the actual risk is without fear clouding your judgement because sometimes you'll be facing the equivalent of a real-life Hannibal Lecter. But most of the time, it's just that David Platt might have scored a goal.

CHAPTER 3

Shit Jobs

I had filled out a nicking sheet and taken it to the Seg unit one morning. As I entered the office I spotted a tube of Steradent denture cleaning tabs.

'Whose are those, then?' I asked, automatically reaching for them.

The officer looked up from his paperwork over his glasses at me.

'I wouldn't if I were you, Dave.'

Something about the tone of his voice made me stop.

'Whose are they?' I asked again, puzzled, my hand in mid-air.

'Hilton,' he said, putting his pen down, taking his glasses off and rubbing the bridge of his nose. 'Or, at least, it was Hilton's arsehole they came out of.'[1]

A shit up

There's no way around it, working in prison, there's a lot of shit to deal with. Don't do it if you've got a phobia of bodily functions. Parcels and packages of every sort of substance the body can produce are flung around a prison

---

1 It turned out that once he had used up his tablets, he had replaced them with three razor blades, two biro inserts, a piece of paper with telephone numbers on and four unidentified tablets.

like confetti at a wedding. We've covered how much claret you encountered, but by far the most popular body product of all was the humble shit. The use of this particular substance as a punishment and a deterrent has been honed to a fine art.

I remember one prisoner who was a bit of an oddity at Parkhurst: a non-violent inmate, a white-collar criminal, who was in for deception and fraud. Polite, well-spoken and highly educated, a university-educated former public schoolboy, who had at one time or another lived the high life. However, the big city salary he earned turned out not to be big enough to maintain his extravagant lifestyle.

The trouble with this particular inmate was that he was the proverbial fish out of water. He didn't mean to piss people off, he just did. The condescending way he spoke to them just rubbed them up the wrong way, the holier-than-thou attitude, the quality clothing, shiny shoes, supremely tidy cell and apparent disdain for his fellow inmates, all made him unpopular. In short, it was decided that he was a posh twat who needed to be taken down a peg or two.

A decision was made that he didn't really deserve a good hiding, slapping or kicking, nor did he warrant a cell trashing so instead it was decided that someone would shit up his cell.

There are, believe it or not, various degrees of shitting up. The worst – a level one shit up, otherwise known as a 'potting' – involves a full container/s filled with accumulated and often multiple donated excrement being thrown around the cell and in particular over personal items such as photos, which leaves the victim's entire cell resplendent in a most unfortunate pebble-dash effect. Then there is the less severe 'warning shot', the 'quick curl down', when someone craps on the bed, on the floor or in a pair of shoes. I'll never forget the first time – I was standing on the landing when a particularly obnoxious inmate came out of his cell, shouting to all and anyone that some cunt has crapped on his pillow and when he finds the cunt responsible, he's a fucking dead man. A 'curling down', which can include pissing on someone's bed, smashing up or burning personal property, is used as a warning for any number of things. It usually works and the debt is normally cleared. However, on the rare occasion that the warning goes unheeded, the punishment will likely escalate into violence of some sort.

In many ways, this particular inmate was fortunate to be on the receiving end of 'only' a quick curl down. But it wasn't going to be on his bed, his floor or in his shoes, no, it was decided that someone would curl one down not on, but inside his pillow. Holding his pillowcase open, the anonymous crafty crapper would crap inside the pillowcase before carefully replacing the pillow neatly on his wonderfully neat and splendidly well-made bed.

It was as expected, not discovered until after bang up, when he went to bed, plumping his pooey pillow ready for a reading session. Only then was the offending article found. To his eternal credit he was savvy enough not to overly react, reluctantly taking the lesson on board and simply informing staff 'that he had a bit of an accident' the following morning.

Honour among thieves

It's a strange thing indeed that with a wing full of criminals, kleptomaniacs, tea leaves and greedy, selfish twats, junkies and the none-too-bright, inmates can ever actually leave their cell doors open, an open invitation to all and sundry. However, in my early years working at Parkhurst, it was a rare thing for an officer to come across a theft from a cell. It happened, of course it did, but it was extremely rare and usually done by a desperately stupid idiot and/or one with a death wish. Usually the only indication staff ever got that a pad thief (an inmate who steals from a cell) had been at work was when someone turned up with their fingers broken. The traditional 'in-house' punishment/warning was usually done by slamming a door on the thief's fingers. However, the massive increase in drug addiction in prisons means that those days are long gone. More likely than not, the modern-day inmate has little or no respect and the desperate junkie nicks stuff simply because he's a desperate junkie.

Shit from above

However bad the volume of faeces is now in the job, it has been far worse. When I first started at Parkhurst, they were in the process of modernising and putting toilets into the cells, but some were still 'slopping out' in the mornings. This led to the well-paid but unpleasant inmate job of 'shit-parcel collector'. I'm sure you can work out what that entailed from the job title but to be specific, it meant walking around the yard, picking up parcels of shit that the inmates had decided to throw out of the window rather than have in a bucket in the corner of their cell overnight. This was more complicated than it sounds as the gap in the windows was extremely small, so inmates would shit into a newspaper, and like a seasoned origami master fold it up as small as possible, put it in a sock and wing it out of the window. Most days, and especially in the summer months, there would be the best part of 100 parcels waiting in the yard. A 'yards party', where an officer supervised the clean-up of the yard, was one of the jobs traditionally reserved for the NEPOs as rats, pigeons and cockroaches picked at the delicious parcels to release their contents as they warmed in the sun. Back then, for an officer to cross the yard was to run the gauntlet of parcels raining down from above. This was just one example of the invisible hierarchy of different sorts of jobs, which experienced officers knew but poor innocent NEPOs were constantly falling foul of.

Early on, one of the jobs I had to do that day was a 'J4'. Juliet 4 was the radio call sign given to the unfortunate sod who had to literally sit on what was, to all intents and purposes, a tennis umpire's chair while being locked in a small, six-foot-by-six-foot, dank, claustrophobic cage, tucked away at one end of a draughty corridor. In front of me was a barred gate, allowing an unobstructed view. My job was simply to observe the inmates that would be attending the library or canteen, both just a few doors down the corridor, and if there was a problem, i.e. a fight, etc., I would raise the alarm.

It wasn't long before the first batch of inmates arrived, and they looked at me, took the piss, rattled the gate and tried to intimidate me. The officers escorting the inmates looked at and ignored me. I tried to ignore everything but failed to ignore the wooden door behind me that was rattling in the wind, wind that was blowing through and freezing cold. Being a slightly naive, ignorant NEPO, I wasn't prepared. I had been told I'd be indoors, so I was only in shirt sleeves – I learned afterwards that staff normally wear a coat, have a flask of something hot and take a magazine (strictly against the rules!). Though don't ever get caught reading it . . .

Exercise on A wing was one of those jobs that was a bit like Marmite – some officers loved to be out on the exercise yard, others hated it. It involved sitting in a small wooden box on the exercise yard, a sort of repurposed garden shed. Occasionally, something would bang on the side of the box and that something was designed to make the NEPO jump, which would of course entertain the inmates for a few minutes.

During the summer months it was great to be out in the yard, but in winter, not so good, so what you found was that the experienced officers ended up doing the job in summer and NEPOs in winter.[2] Later, I found that the hour's exercise was more like an hour's tea break. The experienced old hands went out on to the exercise yard with a small flask of tea or coffee, a couple of bars of chocolate and/or biscuits, a magazine and very often a small radio to listen to the cricket or football ('Don't ever get caught, mind!').

One day early on, when I was a NEPO, it was a freezing cold, dark, dank, pissing down, shitty weather kind of day. The usual practice is to split the exercise session so the poor old officer is only out for half an hour. Once the exercise is called and the inmates rub down searched, the gate is locked and remains that way until the hour is up. I went out to relieve an officer who was a particularly soft touch. They say timing is everything, and on this occasion it certainly was. As soon as he went in and locked the gate, I spotted out of the corner of my eye an inmate known

---

2 Honestly, if you wanted a reliable weather forecast, all you had to do was check first thing to see if NEPOs or more experienced officers were down for exercise.

to all and sundry as 'Numb Nuts' wearing a small green prison-issue towel as a headscarf to protect against the cold and rain. Unfortunately for me, at that exact same time a governor walked through the exercise yard, Numb Nuts stopped doing his press-ups and said, 'Morning, Governor.' The governor nodded and carried on his way. On reaching me, he said, 'Good morning, Mr Berridge,' and as was the normal practice in the good old days, I replied and gave him the exercise roll (told him how many inmates were on the exercise yard). Happy with that, he went on to the wing.

Soon after wrapping up the exercise and securing the gate, etc., I nipped into the tea room to make a quick brew when the wing senior officer popped in and said, 'Dave, can I have a quick word? The governor has just been in and pulled me, wanting to know why the officer – i.e. you – allowed an inmate to have a towel out on the yard and didn't pull him for wearing that towel.' I told him that it was a little bit awkward because even when the governor walked past Numb Nuts, he saw him, acknowledged him and didn't pull him. If the governor didn't see fit to pull him and didn't deem it a serious enough offence to mention it to me then, I couldn't – 'So you'll have to ask the governor why he allowed Numb Nuts to wear a towel, leaving the officer (i.e. me) in an awkward, slightly embarrassing position,' I finished off.

The night shit

Barlow was a confusing inmate: bright as a button and daft as a brush, he rarely spoke to staff or indeed to the other inmates and was generally a bit of a loner. His only real interest, as far as I could see, was to cause disruption. It was never anything serious, direct or confrontational, but somehow always subtle and always annoying. The one time I'd ever seen him lose it was in a rare show of violence when he threw a typewriter at the fish tank. This fish tank was huge, about five feet long, two feet high and twenty inches deep. The toughened glass was no match for the powerful, slightly deranged Barlow. The resulting smash resulted in the ones becoming awash with broken glass, aquarium grit and gravel, ornaments, gallons of water and frantically flapping fish. Barlow just stood there, staring. A couple of staff escorted him to his cell, two of the inmates rescued the now-nearly dying fish, a couple more were running around like overly excited children. Even this incident felt designed to annoy as we were picking up fish tank gravel for weeks. Who throws a typewriter at a fish tank?

Over the course of a summer, staff started noticing a rather horrible sewage-type smell emanating from in or around Barlow's cell. We couldn't find the source of it but with the weather being on the warm side, the smell was becoming an issue. Consequently, the works plumbers were called to try and locate the source, but could find nothing. It was only when the night officer saw Barlow, picking or digging at his cell wall, that the day staff found the source. Over a long period of time Barlow had been repointing his cell using his own excrement as mortar. Bits of the old Victorian brickwork behind his picture board, beneath his bed, etc. had been 'repaired'.[3]

One inmate who was supposedly wheelchair-bound was caught red-handed, shoving faeces and urine out on to the

---

[3] Knowing inmates, I'm surprised Barlow didn't try and invoice us for labour and materials for the work.

landing underneath the door. This inmate was a particularly nasty individual. He claimed that he often needed someone to push his wheelchair as he was not physically able to move himself, however he would often smear excrement on the wheelchair handles, brake lever and wheels.

Biohazard

Even when it wasn't someone deliberately using shit, you still had to have a pretty strong stomach. A particularly unpleasant job was 'clearing a cell', which is when two officers have to clear a recently vacated cell. More often than not, these cells have been left in a terrible state by the none too house-proud previous occupant, who has either been 'ghosted' (removed at very short notice to another prison for security reasons), or taken to the block or chokey (Seg unit). Officers have to go in and clear the cell because every item of kit in the cell must be accounted for. One officer would sit with pen and paper and make a comprehensive list of every single item, while the other officer (usually the NEPO) manhandles each and every item of personal kit into a 'prop bag' (a large strong plastic see-through sack). Once this is done, the bag is sealed with a numbered plastic 'zip tie'.

I remember one particular cell's previous occupant had recently been transferred out to a special secure hospital, owing to his rapidly deteriorating mental health issues. Going into a cell of someone with mental health issues was always going to be an interesting experience. You'd end up praying for the previous occupant to have suffered from OCD, which would at least sometimes be an advantage if the condition manifested itself in obsessive cleaning. Every now and then, the cell would smell half-decent and be extremely tidy. This was not one of those occasions.

As soon as we opened the door, we knew we were in for a treat. It stank to high heaven and somehow managed to look even more disgusting than it smelled. It was quite literally a festering hellhole. The first job was to open the window. The window, however, only opened a matter of inches – the ideal thing would be to have the door open so that any slight breeze might blow through, but this is prison and something as simple as an open door during a cell clearance or search was a definite no-no.

An open cell door would be just too much of a temptation for an inmate, so we always shoot the bolt, close the door and place something behind it, just to give us a warning that the door is being opened.[4]

I started searching the small wooden locker, which was broken and jammed solid with an assortment of soiled stinking clothing, underwear, socks, T-shirts, jogging bottoms and sweatshirts. Thankfully, all of it was prison-issue, so wouldn't have to be accounted for as it was not his 'personal prop' – we could just get rid of it to the laundry, as with all and any 'prison issue' kit, i.e. sheets, pillowcases, towels, etc. Unfortunately, these festering items were so badly encrusted with any number of bizarre bodily stains and secretions, interesting smells, food and who knows what else that they were now little more than a biohazard, which I'm sure were probably more likely to be of interest to a biological warfare laboratory than a laundry.

---

4   This is where a large bolt is locked into place so the door can't actually be locked without an officer releasing the bolt. One of the commandments of being an officer: you always, always 'shoot the bolt' when entering a cell!

There were two pairs of shoes, one of which had at one time or another been a pair of black trainers, but this was pure speculation as they were unlike any trainer either of us had ever seen. The heels on both shoes were crushed flat, most of the tongue had (for whatever reason) been removed and somewhere along the line they had been customised to make them into 'peep-toes' with the ends removed. They were so covered in filth, the actual brand name was a mystery so were recorded as 'one pair of black training-type shoes'. Such a recording is standard practice for a reason. For example, if you were recording the fact that there was a gold ring, it would be listed as 'one yellow metal ring', as would a watch – for example, 'one Omega' or 'one Rolex' – which is recorded as 'one watch with metal strap'. This is simply because the gold may not be gold and the Rolex might just be one of those Far Eastern fakes. However, if you actually put on record the fact that the inmate has a 'Rolex', he'll want a Rolex rather than the Far Eastern fake you must have swapped when you nicked his.

If you're spotting a running theme here, it's true: every single process has to stand up against someone putting a lot of time and effort into coming up with ways to exploit it. In fact, if you wanted to come up with a way of creating a brain trust of all the most devious, cunning and creative minds at breaking and twisting rules, the wings of a prison would be what you'd come up with. It's a cliché that someone goes into prison for one thing and comes out learning how to be more of a criminal, but I've certainly watched it happen first-hand.

Moving on to the toiletries shelf . . . It was packed full of accumulated crap, mainly shampoo sachets and three combs – slightly confusing as this particular inmate had what could best be described as a 'shabby chic' approach to personal grooming. They looked like they'd been dragged backwards through a hedge. In a hurricane.

The toiletries were, like his clothing, prison-issued so could be binned. These included the phallic-shaped, eight-inch shaving stick, with numerous attached pubic hairs and suspect brown streaks. Less easy and slightly more complicated were his numerous boxes and blister packs of medication. We noted down thirteen partially used but unpronounceable and out-of-date medication boxes – these would be returned to Healthcare. There were also five clear plastic containers on the shelf, which were fortunately empty. I say 'fortunately' because my colleague once told me a story about the cell that was searched and the officer found several jars. As he opened one of them for inspection, he made the fatal error of sniff-testing one of the jars, which was packed full of finger- and toe-nail clippings. Though he didn't feel like it at the time, he had had a lucky escape as one of the other jars contained accumulated semen.[5]

Moving on from the inmate's medication, clothing and toiletries, I was stinking and sweating in equal measure. I looked under the bed and found one box of paperwork, a pair of prison-issue slippers, accumulated dust, food, pens, pencils, magazines and newspapers. The stench down there was truly something to behold but it wasn't until I started to strip the bed that we found the source. Apart from the encrusted sheets, which were so filthy, stiff and

5   Apparently, this particular inmate was a witch doctor and 'needed these things for his conjuring'.

stained with every possible type of bodily secretion, pulling them off the plastic-coated mattress produced a sound like parting Velcro. Once I'd done this, we found that there were in fact two mattresses and when we lifted the top one off, we discovered, sandwiched between the two, the now-rancid, putrefying remnants of half-eaten meals, bits of long-forgotten fruit and who knows what else – they certainly didn't put this in the job advert!

Apart from the shoes, an assortment of boxed paperwork and medication, there was nothing that really belonged to the inmate. What there was would likely be binned as it really was not fit for use, including the mattresses and pillows. We got out of there and handed it over to the 'cleaner' (an inmate whose job it was to clean the cell and get it ready for the next occupant). This would certainly not be a quick process as it was decided the cell urgently needed painting (if only to hide the smell) before the next inmate moved in.

Working in prison meant you couldn't be squeamish. It stands to reason that when your world is reduced to one, the size of a prison inmate's internal resources becomes extremely important. In many ways I found it fascinating. You could take away so many of the things outside in society and people would still find ways to create order, meaning and hierarchy – after all, we're just primates, aren't we? In many ways the different levels of a shitting up are a beautiful testament to the human capacity for ingenuity and creativity.

Or maybe just a jar full of shit.

CHAPTER 4

Sex, Drugs and Rock and Roll Call

I was on fours one afternoon doing the roll check, prior to the afternoon unlock. This meant going from cell to cell, looking through the obs panel and checking what was going on in each cell. Everything appeared to be fairly normal, with some of the inmates sleeping, some listening to music, others reading or writing, and a couple, as ever, practising their menacing glare back at me. It was only when I got to the second-from-last cell that things went a little pear-shaped. An inmate called Smith was doing some, to be fair, rather impressive multitasking: standing stark bollock naked, eating a small bread roll while wanking. Willy in one hand, bread roll in the other.[1] He caught my eye but didn't stop – in fact, if anything, he speeded up.

Working in prison, you see pretty much everything and while I have to say that masticating while masturbating was a new one for me, it's certainly not the first time that a prisoner's peculiar urges have come to the fore. If you put a bunch of bored blokes in a room on their own for large portions of the day, what do you expect? It's not for no reason that prisoners' beds are nicknamed 'wank chariots'. But some inmates have a definite knack for wanking during a roll check, the trouble is proving it. I heard the story

---

1 Like a deconstructed hot dog.

of one inmate who during roll check managed to engage the officer in conversation and it was only when halfway through the conversation and the fact that the inmate gave a huge sigh of relief that the officer realised or at least suspected the inmate was not really conversing but actually knocking one out while talking to them. This engaging the unsuspecting officer in conversation has also happened a few times when inmates have weed under the door, wetting the unsuspecting officer's feet.

Another evening, I was doing the roll check on the ones. Opening the observation flap, I saw an image that was one of those images that you can't un-see. Gary Stone was an armed robber and the occupier of this particular cell. However, when I checked the cell, it was most definitely not Stone that I saw wistfully reclining on the bed but what I would later learn was his alter ego, 'Sarah Jane', resplendent in a pink baby doll nightie. He turned and looked at me and carried on reading.

Slightly confused by what I had just seen, or thought I had seen, I finished the roll check and signed to say that the roll was correct. A couple of weeks after this event, Stone was taken to the block, 'on suspicion'. This usually means Security think an inmate is up to no good – he might be hiding something, etc. Whatever the reason, he was to be investigated and he was not happy, shouting the odds, refusing to co-operate and generally being a pain. He was removed under restraint and as per normal practice his clothing was removed (to be searched). It was only then that the staff realised he was wearing a rather fetching set of peach-coloured lingerie.

While Stone was in the Seg unit, another officer and I were tasked with searching his cell. It was the usual procedure of shooting the bolt and putting the chair behind the door to prevent it opening or as a crude warning system in case someone tried to enter while we methodically went through the cell. However, what was not usual was the array of ladies' smalls drying on the heating pipe. It was then that the chair moved and one of the wing's gophers and general dogsbodies poked his head into the cell and said, 'Guv, where's he gone and whose are they?', pointing to the numerous pairs of panties. Time for a bit of quick thinking. We couldn't really say they were his – at that point we didn't know how open Stone was with the wider prison population about what he liked to get up to in the privacy of his cell, or what impact that might have. Equally, we couldn't deny the fact they were there, either. I simply said, 'I think they're souvenirs from his girlfriend.' I hoped that would do it, but from the look on the gopher's face, I was pretty sure that wouldn't be the end of it.

Sex happens in prison in all sorts of contexts. Unlike some other countries, we don't have conjugal visits. I believe in some US prisons there are little huts where husbands and wives are left to become reacquainted. I'm sure there are people agitating for that here but thankfully, as things stand, sex while you're serving time is supposed to be entirely off limits. But of course, that doesn't mean it isn't happening.

Non-consensual sex

There have been various studies over the years that put incidence of rape in prison at somewhere around 1 per cent, but you'll probably have worked out by now that the actual number will be much higher – for a variety of reasons it's massively underreported by inmates. You know it's going on and the one thing that helps prevent it is enough officers to make sure there are eyes on the parts of the prison it could occur in and regular checks. The drop in staffing levels that has occurred over the last decade means reported instances have shot up and the real figure will be much higher.

I remember one infamous arrival at Parkhurst, a serial killer who had tortured and murdered multiple gay men on the outside. Arriving on A wing and obviously keen to 'make an impression', he'd pondered to one of the big boys on the wing what would happen if he started to 'take out' the faggots. I remember at the time thinking this might not be the smartest move in an environment that, even though it was full of homophobia, was equally full of homosexual activity, with often the two things coexisting in the same inmate. Men who would use homosexuality as the greatest insult imaginable, but were regularly involved in sex acts with men and saw no conflict. As I'd thought, his fellow inmates sent him a message and the next time he left his cell, someone set fire to it and burnt him out. It was a pretty clear warning and he was transferred to another prison immediately.

Consensual sex between inmates is officially against the rules but of course, it happens frequently.[2] I'll never forget rushing to the cell of an inmate nicknamed Crusher – a very large, muscular man with a handlebar moustache – only to find another inmate – Scary Mary – being escorted away by another inmate.[3] When we entered the cell, Crusher

---

2   The fact that prisons hand out free condoms is testament to that.
3   Scary Mary was a short, extremely camp inmate, who cut his jeans down to hot pants and twisted his shirts up into crop tops. As you can probably guess, he was also as hard as nails.

was lying on the floor, covered in blood. Scary Mary being in for multiple murders and famously handy with a blade, I put two and two together, raised the alarm and knelt to try and stem the bleeding. Crusher was writhing around on the floor, calling out, 'Please don't take her away from me. Don't split us up, Guv. She's my wife, I love her.'

Nodding along, I was frantically pulling up his claret-soaked T-shirt but unable to find the wounds. When I tried to turn him over to see if he'd been stuck in the back, I saw it: a dented bottle of blackcurrant cordial. I stood up, cautiously sniffing my hands. It turned out during a particularly heated domestic, Scary Mary had battered Crusher to the floor with the delicious blackcurrant drink.

As far as I know, they're still inseparable.

One aspect of sexual activity in prison that always receives a huge amount of coverage in the press is when a prison officer has an affair with an inmate. Over the years it's happened numerous times and understandably always receives a lot of attention.

One day a new female officer arrived at the prison and like most NEPOs, she was full of enthusiasm and confidence. A soon-to-be-married mum, she was bright, bubbly and happy to at last be starting this brand-new career and this new chapter in her life. Her future was decidedly bright. Keen to learn and not frightened of getting stuck in, she made a good first impression (which in itself is hard for any NEPO to do). However, the old hands, the long-serving experienced officers, soon noticed seemingly innocuous clues that things were not quite right. Little things like spending too long talking to a certain inmate, noticing the body language between an inmate and the officer, her spending just a little too long at his door at banging-up time. It could all have been very innocent and insignificant but if there's one thing long-serving prison officers are good at, it's reading people.

So, one of the old hands approached his senior officer and mentioned his concerns. Not to drop a colleague in the shit, but just to make sure everyone was aware. He raised the fact that she was on occasion spending up to forty minutes in one particular cell, at the same time as other inmates were strategically placed on and around the landings – in exactly the place you might put a lookout if you wanted early warning of an approaching officer. When her concerned colleague tried to very gently and diplomatically ask if she was having any problems with the job, whether any of the inmates were giving her a hard time, she reacted angrily, accusing him of trying to mollycoddle her because she was a woman. The SO agreed this was an issue and raised it with one of the managers, only to be told that this sexism had to stop and they needed to stop gossiping about a female colleague. In fact, if it continued, the staff involved could be investigated for sexism *and* bullying. The trouble with this sort of thing is that lots of managers and to a lesser degree certain SOs – usually the ones who now spend limited time working on a wing or landing but an inordinate amount of time in an office – have forgotten the skills that officers on the wing possess.

However, this particular case came to a head when the inmate assaulted another officer, who had also previously been having a relationship with the female officer. The whole complicated, messy, intertwined relationship was then out in the open, both officers were suspended and the inmate transferred to another prison. Only then was the can of worms fully opened and the text messages found. It came out that she had known the assault on the officer was coming and didn't warn him – she had been planning to set him up as being 'corrupt'. She also knew the inmate had a mobile phone and had been texting him risqué messages. In court, the female officer claimed that she had behaved in the way she did to try and glean intelligence from the inmate regarding drugs, mobiles and 'corrupt' staff. In order to gain his trust, she had given him her phone number.

This transgression was at least dealt with when it was discovered. I remember a fellow officer returning to the office to say he was going to have to write up two inmates after finding them in flagrante, or to use his expression 'at it like knives'. He filled in the nicking sheet and the case came in front of the governor. It was expected to be pretty straightforward. After all, how could they dispute what the officer saw? At that time and place the officer witnessed an illegal sex act between inmate A and B. They had been close enough to see the specifics of which organ entered which orifice but both pleaded not guilty. And their defence? Prisoner A had been minding his own business passing the laundry when he had heard the unmistakable sound of someone choking and rushed in to find Prisoner B turning a shade of puce. Luckily, on the outside Prisoner A had received first aid training and swiftly began the Heimlich Manoeuvre. In the chaos and urgency, some of Prisoner A and Prisoner B's clothing had become ruffled, including both of their trousers falling down. Prisoner A did not dispute that his penis had been erect, but stated he had not been aroused.[4] To the astonishment of absolutely everyone, the nicking was thrown out. We all ended up just bloody relieved that he wasn't put up for some sort of medal for quick-thinking bravery.

---

4   I like to think it really is just that exciting to save a life.

Drugs

Drugs are an inescapable part of prison life. Any time you have a bunch of bored, unhappy people looking to escape, they are very often going to look for chemical assistance. Prison, it's the ultimate captive market. So many of the inmates were abusing drugs and alcohol on the outside that it was only natural that it would continue inside. As long as there have been prisons, there have been those who smuggle illegal substances in and those who profit from selling them inside. The misery that criminality around drugs causes on the outside is magnified on the inside. I hate to think how many of the violent acts committed inside were committed either directly or indirectly because of drugs. Inmates desperate to leave their minds would get into debt or carry out favours to fund it.

When I joined, drugs were definitely an issue. Back then, smoking was allowed and very often you'd smell weed hanging in the air. Then there was the odd overdose from someone who had got hold of the stronger stuff – crack cocaine, heroin, methadone and amphetamines but also steroids, prescription painkillers and even epilepsy and heart medicines. Inmates would steal, swap and sell whatever they could get hold of. But in recent years a huge problem has been the flood of synthetic drugs into prisons, the most famous of which is spice.

Spice of life

Spice is a synthetic cannabis and though it has superficially the same effect, it's far more dangerous. Simply put, we all encountered cannabis psychosis from inmates who smoked too much skunk but spice seemed to impact even casual

79

users much more strongly. It was far easier to take too much, induced violence and paranoia, and then the inmates suffered from something which was far more like heroin withdrawal when they couldn't get hold of it.

In a cruel accident of fate, spice entered our prisons seriously around the same time that a raft of biting cuts on staffing levels was hitting the prison system. This led to the lowest levels of staffing at the same time as the largest prison estate we've ever had and a huge increase in substance abuse. A study published in 2022 found that the proportion of inmates who developed a drug problem inside prison stood at about 15 per cent. That doesn't include those who went in with a drug problem already (and, of course, as ever, people who refused to answer).

Hooch

Hooch, or to give its correct title 'illicitly brewed alcohol', is both plentiful and readily available, produced in vast quantities by 'brewers'. It is usually made by mixing fruit water, sugar and bread, all readily available in prisons, mixing it in some sort of container and leaving it somewhere warm so that the miracle of fermentation can take place. The end result often has a higher alcohol content than the spirits you can buy on the outside.[5]

It's used for anything and everything, from the quiet celebration 'soirée', as a currency, coping mechanism, for

---

5 You have to be careful brewing your own alcohol as before it becomes the organic compound ethanol, there is another form of alcohol called methanol, which can cause blindness. It's believed this is where the expression 'blind drunk' comes from.

Dutch courage, a bargaining chip, debt clearing and self-medication. On the outside, a bevvied-up, beyond reason bloke is a potential danger. In prison, it's horrendous. A drunk, often angry, often frustrated inmate is full of bravado and ready for a scrap, with other inmates or staff. Fortunately, it's a problem that other inmates try and deal with themselves because they know that a pissed-up troublemaker will give staff little or no choice but to get involved and get busy – and they really don't want that.

My first experience of hooch was when I inadvertently 'found' a bucketful. Back then, I didn't know what it was, and had never seen or smelt it. However, that one find meant that I would never forget the smell, a distinctive not unpleasant fruity odour. Hooch is relatively easy to make – the difficulty lies in getting hold of the ingredients without anyone noticing and concealing the finished brew.

A master hooch brewer on a wing is both an asset and a popular man. Hooch brewing is very much a team event, as sourcing the ingredients without alerting suspicion is far easier that way. Oranges are the main and bulkiest ingredient and any officer who spots three or four inmates going into a cell with oranges and coming out with sod all is a fairly good indication. Another important readily available ingredient is sugar. The prison supplies inmates with sugar sachets which are often collected – this 'collected' sugar could be a willing donation, stolen, part of a debt or bullied and forced. Another equally important ingredient is a catalyst, a natural yeast to get things going. This can be obtained by letting a small piece of fruit rot or leaving a small piece of bread in an airtight container. Once these ingredients have been collected, containers are needed: either plastic bottles bought from the canteen or scavenged cleaning product containers.

When I started at Parkhurst the policy that was in place for cleaning product containers was 'one for one', i.e. an inmate must hand you one empty container before you hand over another full one, the empty one is disposed of but not before being cut or 'holed' so it can't be used to contain a liquid. I always disposed of any container minus the cap – even the dustbins had a hole in to prevent the storage of liquid. During my last couple of years in the service I saw new officers not only not piercing the container but actually on a couple of occasions handing the container over to an inmate. Putting holes in a perfectly good container was in recent times considered childish and an antiquated practice with only the longer-servicing officers keeping up the practice.

The next problem for the aspiring hooch brewer is maintenance and storage. Maintenance because hooch needs to be kept warm; it must also be bled at regular intervals once the fermenting process is under way. The container will start to swell and if the building pressure is not released intermittently, the whole thing will explode (which is always both entertaining and messy!). It needs to be in a warm place, ideally next to a set of hot pipes, but obviously it must be kept away from prying eyes with the smell as disguised as possible but still accessible for the ongoing maintenance. When an officer walks into a cell and there is an abundance of air fresheners or incense sticks, they should always ask why. Maybe the inmate is undergoing some sort of spiritual awakening but they could also have a massive stash of hooch brewing somewhere in their cell. If there's a bin full of sugar sachets and orange peel and the smell of incense, you've probably found a batch.

An elegant solution is for someone other than the brewer to hold the hooch in their cell for them.

Back then, though, I knew very little about it. I was searching a cell when I found a standard issue slop bucket on the floor of an inmate's locker. I took a quick look and saw what looked like dirty washing-up water in there. It wasn't unusual for inmates to use these buckets to wash their underwear in them. In fact, that was sometimes a lovely gift left when you cleared a cell – a delightful bucket of marinated shitty water. Thankfully, the other officer was a bit more clued up and noticed the bucket. After giving it a sniff, he looked at me and shook his head: 'That's not washing, that's fucking hooch!' It took me a little while to live that down. The inmate just shrugged and said, 'Win some, lose some.'

Very often these small victories were seen as a game, nothing personal. The inmates would get one over on the officers and then the officers would get one over on the inmates. It was rare that these small battles became personal, they were seen as a game that was both played and understood between us and them. On this occasion I placed the inmate on report, but often they would be given a very informal and very unofficial choice: tip the stuff away or be placed on report.

Prison is (and should be in my opinion) an unpleasant environment. At best, it's boring; at worst, it can be terrifying. It's no wonder that inmates seek to escape their reality in any way they can. Plenty of prison officers go to the pub to unwind because of the constant stress. Likewise, you're never going to be able to eradicate that most fundamental human urge of sex.

The problem is that sex and drugs (including alcohol) become a currency, traded as part of a larger web of criminality. In the old days, it was a constant war of attrition in which sometimes the officers won and sometimes the inmates. But (and you'll spot this is a running theme), the low levels of staffing coupled with huge numbers of inmates means that the battle is conceded in many prisons. Huge numbers of prisoners are off their faces on hooch and spice and we simply don't have the resources to stop it. My worry is that at some point, there's going to be one hell of a hangover.

CHAPTER 5

You Don't Have to Be Mad . . .

Freddie Forster was an interesting character. An armed robber and a proper full-blown loudmouth Cockney geezer, full of Cockney wit and confident Cockney charm. He described himself as a 'raspberry' because he had no use of his legs; they were just floppy trouser-filling appendages. He got around the prison on a pair of crutches that on occasion were used as weapons. An armed robber who used crutches, it was certainly different. Forster should have been located in the hospital, where conditions and facilities would have been more convenient for one with his disability, but he refused point-blank to be located with 'the sick, lame and lazy', reasoning that he was a 'proper armed robber, that should be on a proper armed robber's wing'. Quite fearless, he would shout and swear at everyone and anyone, take on all comers. When he 'collected his canteen' or went to the library, he had to walk quite a way, up some steps and along what was once called 'birdcage walk' – a long, covered walkway. Forster was as crafty as he was fearless and often an officer would carry his canteen for him, which could be two or three bags of stuff. He would always hang back while the officer carried his stuff, then when he reached the wing, he would take it from the helpful officer, say 'Thanks, Guv' and hobble back on to the wing, crutches and bags swinging all over the place. He proceeded to inform everyone that 'these fucking kangas, wouldn't even carry the raspberry's canteen'. It was a weekly standing joke.

One day I arrived on the wing just in time to see Big Dave putting Forster in one of the chest freezers, Forster having pissed him off once too often. Dave decided to stick him in a freezer rather than beat the shit out of a raspberry – after all, it wasn't really the done thing to beat up a cripple. Luckily for Forster, the freezer was nearly full. I arrived to see Dave trying to use Forster's arse to shuffle the frozen things out of the way so that he could get him deep enough into the freezer to close the lid, but he wasn't having much success and was getting frustrated. We watched him try a couple more times before rushing in to get Forster out. He was fine, if a little chilly, and still shouting the odds.

On the outside, trying to put a disabled person in a freezer would probably, understandably, see questions asked of your mental health. However in prison, it was just another Tuesday.

Mental health is a massive issue in prisons. At any one time about 10 per cent of the prison population is receiving active treatment and I read recently that it's been estimated 70 per cent of inmates have some form of mental health need at some point. Now that needs to come with a massive and familiar caveat. I am in no way disputing that there are some inmates with serious mental health issues and if they didn't have these issues when they went in, then I can see why they might develop them, if only because they might abuse one of the many substances mentioned in the previous chapter. However, mental health is just another angle that inmates know they can work to their advantage. If you can get drugs and time out of your cell for hearing voices in your head, then inmates will say they hear voices. Like everything else in prison, there is always a risk that some of the most streetwise people on the planet will abuse the rules that are put in place in good faith to try and help.

To give just one example: C wing, the secure mental health unit where I met some of the most frightening inmates, was overseen by a psychiatrist called Dr Bob Johnson, whose methods were controversial. Now bear in mind that this is only my opinion and Dr Johnson pretty much has more degrees than I've had hot dinners. Described as 'an intellectual maverick', he had set about treating the inmates under his care with a single-minded determination to find out what event in their childhood was key to understanding their later behaviour. So what happened? Quite quickly, many inmates began to remember key events and coincidentally those 'events' were exactly the sort he was looking for. It's perfectly possible that he had uncovered the key to it all, but I would also ask whether it was possible that some of the most manipulative and cunningly intelligent people you could ever meet might have worked out a way to leverage the situation to best suit themselves. All I know is that I once overheard three inmates discussing the best way to tell Johnson a bullshit story that would mean he would up their meds, which they could then sell on for a tidy profit.

So they went to see him and he upped their meds. To him, I'm sure it seemed as if the prison staff simply didn't understand the complexity of what he was trying to do. To us, it seemed naive not to make the most of those who had so much combined experience of prisoner behaviour. We would never have tried to argue with him about psychiatry. But prisoners? Prisoners we knew about.

That said, there were some positive results, including a reduction in the number of assaults and wing emergencies among the prisoners he treated.[1]

There was a constant battle waged as inmates tried to seize any advantage they could, every rule potentially something they could utilise. One of the worst offenders was a guy called Brian Lawrence. A retired teacher, he had bludgeoned to death a friend of his ex-lover, with whom he had become obsessed, then hired a hitman to kill two other love rivals. In my opinion, he wasn't an enhanced inmate. He was just an arsehole. Lawrence had the most well-developed superiority complex of anyone I'd ever met and believed that prison staff were a lower form of pond life. He only spoke in multisyllabic words but loved the sound of his own voice; he was constantly quoting the rules and regulations at you too.

Several weeks after Lawrence had moved to C wing, he was caught bang to rights planning an audacious escape. His rather desperate attempt was discovered by staff, the selfsame lower form of pond life staff, who found his 'plans' – which were written in lemon juice and using a coded form within sudoku puzzles, along with maps and details on how to bring a helicopter over to the Isle of Wight and which areas of the prison weren't heavily protected by anti-helicopter wires. The whole thing was scheduled and planned to be carried out during the Isle of Wight's annual summer music festival when air traffic, road traffic and the policing on the island were stretched to their limit. Lawrence was really pissed off, believing his intellectual superiority had allowed him to plan an audacious, foolproof escape plan. The fact that the prison officers had caught him so very

---

1   https://www.independent.co.uk/news/the-predators-1280220.html

easily, prison officers that he had hitherto considered to be a vastly inferior species who had in fact outsmarted this would-be criminal mastermind, would have infuriated him. Soon afterwards he was transferred out to another prison.

Self-harm

I was in the office doing paperwork one day when the radio sprang to life with a Seg unit officer asking for assistance. It was a code red, which means 'blood', and for an officer to ask for assistance means it's serious. A couple of us made our way to the Seg and one of the cleaners pointed to where the incident was, which happened to be in the end cell on the ones. An inmate was sitting on the bed with an officer apparently kneeling in front of him. The poor officer was desperately trying to staunch a deep nasty-looking cut to the inmate's right calf – he had sliced through it and sliced deeply. This inmate was calmly explaining that he does this quite regularly, but this time had 'fucked it up a bit'. He had, he said, been carving himself up for months without ever telling anyone and the reason he did his legs was because he could hide the injuries under his trousers. Self-harming by stealth was quite common and often we wouldn't know about it until they went too far. This time the injury was serious enough for him to be taken to the local hospital.

Prisoners would often cut themselves and rub dirt or shit into the wounds so it would become infected and they'd need a trip to the hospital. As ever, who knew the exact balance of genuine mental health issue, an attempt to get out of their cell for a day out, plus generally fucking with the system? Any time we had to move an inmate was a horrendous logistical endeavour and they knew it. Causing any sort of disruption, however small, was a tiny victory in the ongoing war between inmate and screw.

One day an inmate came into the wing office and showed the officer sitting at the desk a self-inflicted cut, which he had just done. The three cuts were superficial, nothing to get excited about. The inmate went on to, or at least tried to, explain himself and the reasons for cutting himself. At this point the officer rolled up his sleeve and said, 'I know exactly how you feel – I did these yesterday.' There on his left arm was a large bandage covering wounds that were sort of seeping. The officer went on to explain he had been self-harming for months. It was the only time I'd ever seen an inmate on the back foot where this was concerned.

Incident at height

The ultimate act of self-harm you encountered was suicide. Sadly, officers experienced inmates who have killed themselves any number of times and those self-same officers have managed to stop suicidal inmates being successful many times more. For all sorts of reasons, suicide is more common in prison than in the general population. It was always a solemn occasion.

I remember one night, we had just finished banging up the wing after a hugely busy shift spent responding to five alarm bell situations on a Saturday afternoon. Usually you could bank on Saturdays being one of the quieter days with a bit of exercise, some family visits and football on TV, but not today. The only good thing was that two of the bells were resolved before we got there, one was false and the two others, though genuine fights, were quickly brought under control. Best of all, I had managed not to do any of the loathsome paperwork.

As soon as we had signed for the roll and informed the control room that the wing was secure and the roll was correct, we were asked to attend another wing as there was an ongoing incident.

No one wants to hear those words.

An inmate was threatening to kill himself and had decided, presumably to cover all bases, to put a noose around his neck and jump from the top landing. Fortunately, the suicide netting is there to prevent just such an attempt and or to catch any poor soul who has been thrown off a landing by someone else.[2] The inmate had placed himself right above the bottom step. This wasn't a particularly long drop, though the fact that he was wearing a noose obviously meant some potentially fatal injuries could occur. The noose on this occasion was wire (cut, we later found, out from one of the wing freezers). I say 'on this occasion' because noose-wearing in a prison is a common occurrence and the material used can have important messages. In my experience if it's made from thin strips of bed sheets, it's more likely to be a cry for help as this sort of improvised noose is highly likely to break. However, as in this case, if wire/flex or material has been twisted over and over again to form some kind of tough rope, it's much more likely to be a serious attempt. They had sent a female officer whom the inmate got on particularly well with to try and form a dialogue with him.[3]

---

2 Believe me, this netting gets a lot of use.

3 There would always be an official appointed negotiator on call but often it worked better if it was someone the inmate had a positive relationship with.

Half a dozen mattresses were collected from the stores and put on the stairs immediately below the suicidal inmate, with medics with wire cutters on standby. The IMB officers were discreetly positioned too.[4] Fortunately, the inmate soon started talking or rather complaining – apparently, all this was because a 'bag of prop' hadn't arrived at the prison, consequently he felt the need to teach us a lesson, which was to threaten or commit suicide. After about forty minutes and plenty of assurances from the custodial manager (CM) regarding his missing bag, he decided to come down but owing to the fact that he couldn't undo the knot he had tied, he had to wait for the CM to come and help untie it.

The postscript to the inmate's 'suicide attempt' was that his bag had somehow and inadvertently been lost (it's not unusual for this to happen) and he was eventually compensated for the loss of his property. Compensation paid to inmates within the prison system is commonplace and more often than not, the enterprising inmate can make a tidy profit by slipping, falling, tripping and lying, losing stuff, breaking stuff, including mail and receiving the wrong medication can all be potentially profitable sources of income.

There were inmates who were under treatment or being assessed but also a whole host of inmates who, while not being formally diagnosed, were, in our unqualified opinion, 'fucking mental'.

---

4 Independent Monitoring Boards are made up of over 1000 unpaid volunteers operating in every prison in England and Wales, as well as every immigration detention facility across the UK. They are there to observe and ensure prisoners are being treated fairly and humanely.

The pencil is mightier . . .

An inmate was taken to a local hospital to have a pencil removed from his penis. Normally, the penis was the thing being inserted but apparently the inmate had taken to doing this regularly (which gives a whole new meaning to having lead in your pencil). However, this time his enthusiasm got the better of him and he couldn't get the thing out. The hospital managed and it was apparently an HB2.

Another slightly odd incident that happened on the wing was when an inmate who was fairly young was seen leopard crawling along one of the landings. Entertaining, but odd as this was, it became less funny when it was realised that the inmate was stark bollock naked and crawling along the old wooden landing floor (the potential for a splinter catching a delicate dangling piece of privates was very realistic), clutching a plastic knife in his teeth. One of the longer-serving officers approached the inmate, standing above him, thinking this would bring the whole crazy scene to an end. It didn't even break his rhythm; he carried on and just crawled around the officer, still holding the piece of plastic cutlery firmly between his teeth. It was only at this point that the laughter ceased. Refusing or unable to engage with the staff, he was gently guided into the recess area, Healthcare and the psychology department were called and he was taken to the prison hospital. It transpired that he had had a history of mental illness and was then 'ghosted out' (removed and transferred to another prison) and he apparently committed suicide soon after.

Toast of the town

One day, the wing idiot was seen coming out of his cell on the twos landing, having been beaten black and blue with a chunk of ear missing. He claimed to have slipped in his cell, which was so obviously untrue, but the fact that he had slipped and banged his head and had not, as we so wrongly assumed, been beaten up meant that for us, a shedload of paperwork was now unnecessary. He didn't want to go to the hospital but said he had now finished with the iron and ironing board! Later, we found out that he had, in fact, been ironing the bread, holding the hot iron on the bread until it toasted or at least went a bit crispy.

When the other inmates heard about this, he was in deep shit and consequently taught a lesson. Inmates often use the wing iron and ironing board just before a visit to find that he had not only fucked up the iron but had the officers seen him do it, the ironing facilities would have been withdrawn. As a result of his selfish stupidity, he was very unpopular and very much in the shit.

A few days after the wing idiot slipped and fell in his cell while ironing toast, one of the prison electricians came on to the wing, pushing a sack truck (two-wheeled trolley) containing a large box and a bag of tools. Being a bunch of nosy twats, we asked him what was in the box. He informed us that each and every wing was to have a toaster installed on the landing for the inmates to use. We knew he was taking the piss because the box was way too big and besides, the staff tea room had been waiting nearly three months for a toaster. He assured us that the governor had given the works department clear and concise instructions that each and every wing within the prison was to have a toaster installed. To prove it, he unpacked a Dualit DCT three-slice conveyor toaster, the type of industrial-size toaster that you would normally find in the breakfast area of a decent hotel, costing hundreds of pounds. Letting inmates loose with a toaster could only end in tears. Just looking at it, you could see about twenty different parts that could be dismantled and used to make weapons, wedged into door locks so we couldn't get in, or otherwise used to make everyone's lives a misery.

The governors were informed that this might not be a good idea. However, they told us that it could only be a positive, beneficial thing and make things more relaxed – 'after all, everyone likes a relaxing round of tea and toast' – and as long as we monitored and switched the toaster off prior to bang up, what could possibly go wrong? Sometimes some governors show such a wonderful degree of naivety that would in normal circumstances be rather touching, but on a wing full of inmates, it's just plain stupid. But the governors had been very clear, so in they went.

On the first morning the toaster was installed, a fight broke out because someone decided to have four pieces of toast, which had taken too long. He was apparently told by another inmate that he was taking the piss and holding everyone up. After shrugging his shoulders, he got a slapping. The following day, an argument occurred because someone's toast wasn't quite golden brown enough so he put it through a second time, which also pissed people off. A couple of late risers eventually got out of their wanking chariots and tried to use the toaster just as staff were switching it off in readiness for sending the inmates out to work. They were informed that they were too late and not being morning, people started ranting and raving, mentioning their human rights, racism and fairness, etc., before one knocked the toaster on to the floor, which incidentally we didn't actually mind because we now contacted the works department, explained what had happened and asked if they could come and collect it to fix it or replace it – 'oh, and that there was no actual need to hurry'.

It took four weeks to get the toaster back on the wing. When finally reinstalled, it was only for three days before it was removed because some greedy twat tried to put too many pieces of bread in, jamming the whole thing, which resulted in the toast burning, the smoke detectors automatically raising the fire alarm and staff enthusiastically using fire extinguishers to douse the smoke (no flames, just smoke), which once again rendered the toaster useless. The works department were again called to take the toaster away to be replaced or repaired. On this occasion it had to be replaced, not because of smoke damage but because of the damage caused by the fire extinguishers. It took a couple of goes for everyone to work out that this sort of toaster wasn't a good idea.

If only someone had told them that to begin with.

Sweeties

Kevin, it would be fair to say, was not an overly intimidating physical specimen. A little over five foot three inches, he weighed somewhere between eight and eight and a half stone. From a distance, he looked like a shy, slightly sulky, withdrawn twelve-year-old. However, this first impression was misleading because when provoked or he lost his temper, he became an extremely intimidating presence, becoming violent and quick to anger. He once had to be restrained by six officers when he'd become angry and even then, it took ages to get him under control again.

When I had started on C wing, I was given the rundown, the who's who, etc., and I remember that when Kevin's name was mentioned, they said not to underestimate him. They told me of the time that it took six officers to hold him down and control him and this was only done with a great deal of effort and experience. He was strong when his temper was lost. But this particular morning when he approached me, he seemed to be in a good mood.

'Mr B?' he called out.

Normally in a situation like this, I would read the signs, the expressions and mannerisms; these tiny clues should under normal circumstances give at least a small indication of what was about to happen. Was he pissed off, about to get arsey, in a good or bad mood and more importantly, had he taken his meds?

'Mr B?' he asked, 'are you any good at spelling?'

Now this is the sort of question from an inmate that it's always hard to know how to answer. Is it a trick? If I say yes, is he going to ask me how to spell antidisestablishmentarianism? I decided to err on the side of caution.

'Well, Kev, whatever it is, I'm sure I can give it a go. Fire away.'

He looked back at me gratefully.

'Kid.'

I was sure it was a wind-up.

'Kid?'

But he just kept looking at me with his open, child-like face.

So, I showed willing.

'K.'

He nodded.

'I.'

Again, he nodded.

'D.'

He nodded once more.

'Could you write it down for me?'

Still not entirely convinced it wasn't a wind-up, I wrote each letter out. And just to err on the side of caution I said, 'I think that's how it's spelt.' After he was sort of satisfied, he thanked me again, reached into his pocket and held his hand out. In it was a boiled sweet. It looked as if it had been in his trouser pocket for weeks, sat on, sucked and re-wrapped. Not the sort of thing you'd want to eat. However, I didn't have the bottle to say no to his face – who knows how he'd react?

'Er, thanks, Kevin. I'll have it later if that's OK?'

He beamed, nodded and went off down the corridor.

The following day, just after unlocking the wing, I went down to make the brews. When I returned to the twos landing, I saw Kevin talking to my colleagues. I wondered if he'd lost the bit of paper and forgotten how to spell kid. I was carrying the brews or I would have sneaked back down and left my colleague to it. Unfortunately, Kevin spotted me and smiled as I placed the brews down.

'Morning, Kevin,' I said.

He smiled again, before replying, 'Morning, Mr B, I've brought you something.'

Now this was never a sentence you wanted to hear from an inmate, especially one as volatile as Kevin. I had visions of him opening his fist to reveal some sort of body part. But it was then that Kevin handed me another sweet and again it looked as if it had been in his trouser pocket for a fortnight and been through the washing machine, and his sweaty, clammy mitts had been holding the thing for too long and too tight. Unfortunately, I was once again in a bit of a dilemma, even more so than the last time Kevin offered me a sweet. That one had been a run-of-the-mill, basic, red, hard-boiled sweet. Now he was offering me the crème de la crème of sweets, a Cadbury's Chocolate Eclair, to which I have to admit I was rather partial. Even so, there was no way I was going to eat it. However, my continuing lack of courage prevented me from not taking it and so, with a degree of reluctance, I took it. I could see my colleagues watching me, trying to keep a straight face.

'Thank you, Kevin.'

'It's for helping me yesterday, he said. Then nodded before adding, 'With the spelling.'

'Any time, mate.'

He left and I could hear the sound of laughter from my delighted colleagues.

'Awww! It's nice you've got a little friend to share your sweets with.'

'Fuck off!' I said and very quietly, put the sweet in the bin.

CHAPTER 6

Escapism (and Other Fuckups)

One January morning, in 1995, a few years into my time at Parkhurst, I had a day off. I was in town doing a bit of shopping when I spotted a colleague and crossed the road to say hello. I was already curious because he was wearing his uniform, which is something no Parkhurst prison officer would ever normally do.[1] And it was half ten in the morning, too late to be finishing a night shift or starting a morning shift, and too early to be starting an afternoon shift.

'All right there,' I said. 'Starting or finishing?'

He just looked at me as if I was mad.

'Haven't you heard? The escape has fucked all the shifts. I've just finished a twenty-hour shift.'

'Escape?'

We stood in the street and he filled me in on how this 'complete and utter clusterfuck' had happened the previous day. It turned out that three inmates, Keith Rose, Matthew Williams and Andrew Rodger – two murderers and a bomb-making arsonist – had escaped. Thank fuck I hadn't been working the day before either! They had apparently

---

1 Strangely, I've noticed that the younger generation of prison officers don't have this concern and are much more comfortable wearing their uniforms out in public. I have no idea why, or what this means, but it's a definite generational thing.

escaped from the gym after the evening session, got over the five-metre high fencing and walls using tools and equipment including a ladder they had methodically fashioned over a long period of time. It was rumoured they had even been able to make a replica gun and a working key.

It later transpired that their plan was to steal a plane from a small airfield a few miles from the prison, as one of the inmates was a qualified pilot. However, once over the perimeter wall, they very quickly realised that they were, to use a technical term, fucked. Their meticulous planning might have got them over the wall and out of the prison, but getting out and staying out would prove to be two entirely different things. For them, the hard part was only just starting. As the entire island went on high alert so they went to ground.

Much has been written about the escape in the newspapers, with documentaries made and various theories bandied about, culminating in a scathing official report written by Sir John Learmont, a retired British army general, so I won't go into a huge amount of detail here. My feeling is that of all the thousands of words produced, the reports and articles and documentaries, not many of them were by people who were actually there. Consequently, the story about what went so very wrong which was told to the public was told by those looking to assign blame. For example, I remember colleagues who submitted SIRs about one of the inmates.[2] On more than one occasion he was seen on the exercise yard, pacing

---

2 In those days an SIR (Security Information Report) was submitted by concerned staff indicating any behaviour that could be detrimental to the security of the prison.

out distances, looking up at cameras, standing in certain areas for periods of time. At the time we thought he was or could be checking for possible camera blind spots. We were told that this was just 'him being him'. More than once staff were instructed not to submit so many reports and not to keep using words and phrases like 'bizarre behaviour' and 'up to something'.

At this point, remember, Parkhurst was basically a building site and had been since before I had arrived in 1992, as the wings were slowly being refurbished and brought up to date. We were told that during this time the governor had made numerous attempts at getting improved perimeter security but had apparently been met with a degree of resistance. This would all have been happening many levels above my head, but I can imagine a scenario in which there was a resistance to spending even more money on Parkhurst during this period. Probably from exactly the same people who would then drive the investigation into what had gone wrong.

For example, much was made of the amount of time that passed before the alarm was first raised. My under-standing is that D wing staff knew something was wrong almost immediately. The officer on the roll board realised that there were three inmates unaccounted for. However, it's not uncommon for there to be a bit of a faff with the numbers, i.e. counting and accounting for the correct number of inmates in the correct place at the correct time. When this does happen, it usually only takes five to ten minutes before every inmate is accounted for so staff were dispatched to confirm the whereabouts of the three missing inmates. Cells were checked, association, khazis and every other nook and cranny.

Several minutes later, and with no one managing to confirm their exact location, procedure kicked in and there was the call for an immediate wing bang up, known as a 'stand fast roll check'. Twenty minutes later and still no sighting. It was now officially panic stations time and after about forty-five minutes or so, it was clear that a possible escape was in progress. The shit hit the fan and all hands were now very much on deck. The alarm was raised and the prison was put into immediate lockdown. All gates were frozen and no one but no one was allowed to enter or leave the prison. This was unfortunate because apparently the duty governor was not in the prison at the time and when the shit hit the fan or to use the correct and more formal terminology, the alarm was raised, he tried to enter the prison but couldn't because the whole place was in complete lockdown.

Staff were briefed, as were the police. Some staff were to search the inside of the prison, others were given various locations known as 'fixed posts', strategically located around the island. And so it was that groups of three officers were now, much like the group of three escaped inmates, wandering around the island. A police helicopter complete with infrared night vision cameras had been seconded to help with the search and they were given what seems like it should have been the relatively easy job of looking for a group of three individuals wandering around the Isle of Wight on a freezing January night. However, this turned out to be anything but easy, because of the numerous groups of three prison officers on the ground. It turned out while the helicopter was very good at finding prison officers, it had been rendered effectively useless by the search parties.

Some prison officers ended up in the middle of nowhere, with nothing to eat, nothing to drink, radios in short supply and even if they had one, the battery life of those old radios meant they didn't last through the night. Eventually though, after five days, the escaped prisoners were found not far from Parkhurst but not before they'd caught a taxi and tried to steal the aircraft and several boats.

Successful prison escapes are very rare,[3] but understandably, they always get a huge amount of attention. People have those famous escapes in mind, like the Great Train Robber, Ronnie Biggs, from Wandsworth in 1965, who climbed the wall with a rope ladder and escaped in a removals van, before spending thirty-six years on the run. They love the stories of improvised tools, of decoy bodies made from papier mâché and replica guns made using a bar of soap. But most inmates, most of the time, aren't plotting their escape – and the ones who are plotting are almost never successful.

I remember one attempt at Parkhurst, where inmates managed to remove the old Victorian bricks without anyone hearing and would likely have got away with it but at the last minute had a loud argument about where they should go. It was this argument that alerted the officers. The truth is that a UK prison is incredibly difficult to break out of and almost impossible to stay broken out of. This was

---

3 The UK government consider a prisoner to have escaped if they breach the secure perimeter of a closed prison or overcome the control of the escorting staff for longer than fifteen minutes, or commit an offence before fifteen minutes. Using this definition, over the last five years, there have been ten 'escapes' across the whole of the prison estate.

especially true of Parkhurst, where getting off the island itself was an extra element to any escape and something we were constantly guarding against.

Rogue Elephant

I was once working in the Emergency Control Room (ECR), which is the hub of the prison – the nerve centre – and just about everything is run from there. The movement of all and anything is done through the control room. This super-secure room has banks of cameras covering the entire prison. All and any movement through the prison must be cleared and authorised by the control room and a number of gates within the prison can only be unlocked by the control room operator. This will only be done once ID has been confirmed and cleared.

One of the weekly jobs done by the control room staff was to carry out a test call for 'Rogue Elephant'. Operation 'Rogue Elephant' was an emergency system put in place to intercept any possible use of aircraft that might be used to aid in the escape of an inmate (or inmates). Once a week at a given time a coded phone call would be made to a nominated RAF station on the mainland. The caller would call a special, super-secure emergency hotline and simply say, 'Operation Rogue Elephant test call'. All very cloak-and-dagger stuff. However, should the caller not say 'test call', it would be assumed that this was a genuine call and the RAF would do whatever it was that the RAF do in this eventuality (basically, scramble the aircraft that would then intercept the potential escape).

This particular day the test call was due. The phone call made, the caller waited, but there was no answer. This was unusual but immediately a second call was made and then after a few rings, the phone was answered. The usual procedure followed: 'Operation Rogue Elephant, test call'. A slight pause followed by the seemingly confused individual. Who simply said, 'I'm sorry, I just heard the phone ringing and picked it up. I don't know anything about old elephants, I'm just the cleaner and I've been on holiday!'

No more cat A

The Parkhurst escape came only a few short months after the Whitemoor escape, where six inmates, including five IRA members, had smuggled in guns and Semtex and escaped from their special secure unit (SSU). They were recaptured within minutes but two escapes from two high-security prisons in quick succession was never going to be a good thing and consequently Parkhurst lost its cat A status despite the many millions of pounds recently spent to refurbish it into a modern cat A prison with hundreds of cat A cells. I was slightly shocked as I had thought the fact that Parkhurst was on an island with the sea around us as the final barrier to escape would always stand it in good stead.

Along with the loss of cat A status went the SSU, the super-secure special secure unit that had first opened in 1966. The SSU tended to house prisoners who were an increased risk of escape because of their connections to some sort of organisation on the outside. In practical terms, this meant mainly big-time armed robbers and terrorists. Prior to my arrival at Parkhurst, one of the Krays had been located in the SSU, as had the notorious armed robber, kidnapper and multiple murderer Donald Neilson, known as 'the Black Panther', Valerio Viccei, the playboy bank robber and mastermind behind the £62m Knightsbridge safe deposit raid, Brian Robinson, one of the brains behind the 1983 Brink's-Mat armed robbery, which netted the robbers £23m (Micky McAvoy, another one of the armed robbers, was also in Parkhurst but on D wing).

They tended to be big hitters. Wayne Hurren was another inmate in the SSU, who was serving twenty years for shooting three police officers. His nickname was apparently 'John Wayne' because he always carried two guns and at one time was called 'public enemy number one'. He was unpredictable and very slippery, especially when he covered himself in baby oil, which he liked to do whenever getting into a bit of a tear-up with officers. Hurren was just as dangerous to the public in prison as he was on the outside and had once arranged from prison to have minicab driver David Foley killed because he had assaulted Hurren's wife, Pamela. The whole arrangement for his death was recorded on prison phones. Hurren knew, as does every inmate, that all phone calls are monitored and recorded, but such was his thirst for revenge that caution seemingly went out of the window. The recordings planning the shooting of Foley in King's Cross were used in the court case that followed and amounted to some 220 pages of transcript.

On the move

When the SSU closed down, we had to relocate the inmates. A few staff were picked or were volunteered for this job and I was detailed to be on an escort taking two of the IRA terrorists to one of the cat A dispersal prisons on the mainland. It was a type of escort that was new to me. I had, of course, done a few cat A escorts before but this was on a different scale. For a start, we would be on a secure police lorry as opposed to the usual prison cat A van and on board would be two Metropolitan Police officers along with the driver and navigator. The escorting prison staff would be in the back along with the inmates: two discipline officers, two SOs and a PO, making seven staff for two prisoners. Along the route, we would be accompanied by armed police outriders, clearing the way and making sure we arrived at our final destination. There was serious concern that the van would be attacked by IRA members, supporters or sympathisers.

It was an early morning start, in part to avoid the rush-hour traffic. We searched the vehicles and prisoners thoroughly and once the paperwork was done, it was all aboard and clear to go. The massive prison vehicle gates were opened to armed police and police vehicles waiting outside in the prison car park. It was like something out of a Hollywood film. They were clearing the way, holding back the traffic, blue flashing lights informing everyone to clear the way. We sped to the ferry in a fraction of the time it would normally take and once on, were given about a third of the ferry to ourselves, surrounded by police vehicles and armed police.

The first part of the drive would take us to a police station in the Home Counties. There, we'd have a quick toilet stop, a cup of tea and change the police escort. Leaving there, it was north to a prison in the midlands, where we would stop for lunch and again pick up another set of armed police escorts. In spite of the escorts and the manpower it was hard not to pay attention to every bump in the road.

Once the midlands stop was over and the prisoners were once again safely aboard the police lorry, we left for the last leg of the trip. Unfortunately, getting out of this prison in our lorry was a bit of a squeeze and the driver was experiencing some difficulty in manoeuvring. While reversing out and around a tight corner, he gently clipped a wall. A loud metallic screeching and crunching echoed its way through the vehicle. In the back, the two inmates laughed hysterically at the perceived ineptitude of it all, shouting, 'The driver's fucking drunk!'

Once clear of the prison though, it was a straight run to our final destination. We finally arrived late afternoon and were waved straight through to the reception area. It was only now that the full extent of the prison wall-scraping incident became apparent. The exit door on the side of the vehicle had unbeknown to us been slightly bent and warped and now couldn't be opened. The police tried and we tried, they pulled, we pushed, pushed and kicked the bloody thing, all to no avail. The prisoners were wetting themselves with laughter, laughing at the irony that five prison staff were desperately trying to break out of a super-secure police vehicle inside a maximum high-security prison. Fortunately for us, there was an 'emergency only' escape hatch in the roof of the thing. We were in the process of working out how to reach the rooftop hatch when we were finally and thankfully extricated. Embarrassed and slightly red-faced but relieved when the door was opened, courtesy of the prison works department with a small jar of elbow grease and a rather large crowbar!

Though an actual escape was rare, the sheer volume of prisoners we were moving about every day left plenty of opportunity for more minor mistakes – or what we would like to call fuckups.

Fuckups

I was working on one of the wings and busy banging my landing up, the threes. I had just got the last one away when I realised that some idiot had either left the threes' shower on or worse, some idiot was still in there. When I went in, I saw that the shower had been tied on using a shoelace. I removed the shoelace and had returned to the landing when a voice from above shouted down to me, ''Ere, Guv, you banging us up or what?' Slightly confused, I asked where the officer was – 'He's fucked off and left me out' was his reply. I went up and banged the inmate up and then went down to the ones to sign the roll book to say my roll was correct while asking who had banged up the fours. The answer was an officer who very quickly had become familiar to me.

'Where is he?' I asked.

'He's signed up and fucked off,' was the answer.

Now, some aspects of the job can be difficult. There are entire aspects that need years to really develop. However, signing the book to say that all the prisoners are in their cells without checking that you've actually left one of them in the shower blocks is pretty fundamental. It's exactly this sort of moment that could be leveraged into an escape attempt. Luckily, this particular inmate wasn't so minded. I let this officer know our esteemed mutual colleague had 'left one out' but that I'd put him away.

'For fuck's sake,' he said, 'that's about the fourth time he's done that!'

Shots fired

Lunchtime is quiet time. An opportunity for officers either to go to the gym, sleep, snooze or catch up on paperwork. In days gone by, it was the time when they would more often than not partake in the traditional liquid lunch. However, with the closure of many of the prison clubs, this doesn't happen nearly as much as it used to. I remember very early on at Parkhurst a couple of officers who had come back from lunch a lot louder, a lot braver and a lot more enthusiastic than they had been in the morning.

One lunchtime, I was rudely interrupted by the general alarm going off. Normally this would only ever happen if inmates were out and about, so as they were all banged up, the alarm was surprising. The simple transmission was 'Code red Charlie wing, any available staff to attend'. I and several other staff from around the prison made our way to C wing and were immediately directed to the threes, where O1 was at a cell door, trying to talk to the inmate in the cell. Two things were working against O1 (well, three if you count the inmates' fury), one was that the inmate spoke no English and two, he had what appeared to be a small calibre bullet wound smack bang in the middle of his forehead. You didn't have to be a genius to imagine the volume of shit that would hit the fan if it turned out someone had made or smuggled a working gun into the prison. Part of me would have been impressed with whoever had managed to fit that in their prison wallet. Guns being smuggled into prison wasn't entirely unknown of course but still there would be massive questions asked. Apart from anything else, how had someone shot him while he was banged up? Had he shot himself?

'What's happened here then?' I called to him.

'I'm fucked if I know,' said O1. 'He can't speak English and is clearly off his tits on something. He just keeps shouting at me.'

And it was true, he was shouting the same thing again and again. His cell was a mess, broken furniture and blood everywhere. If he did have a gun in there, we were going to have to get in there and restrain him. He had picked up one of the broken bits of furniture and was waving it about the cell.

When the medics arrived and there was enough staff, we entered the cell. He stopped waving the wood about, sat on his bed and started to cry. It turned out that it wasn't a bullet wound at all but after smashing up his furniture, he'd decided to hit himself in the head with one of the bits of wood, only it had a screw sticking out of it, which had got stuck in his forehead and when he'd pulled it out, had torn a neat round hole in his head. He was taken to the Healthcare Centre and we never did find out what set him off, or why he was threatening to brain himself.

Handcuffs at front!

One morning, I had just dropped off half a dozen cat A books to the gym and was just returning to the wing when the radio blurted out, 'Alarm bell Alpha, alarm bell Alpha'. I was pretty close and made my way there. As I arrived, the officer in the wing office who was talking on the phone, pointed up and said the alarm was on the threes so I made my way up and was just climbing the last few stairs when I heard the unmistakable sound of a scuffle. I was on the second step from the top when I looked ahead and saw within touching distance the back of a white shirt rapidly approaching, coming down the steps towards me. Instinctively, I raised my arms and pushed forwards to try and stop us both toppling down the steep flight of steps, then grabbed hold of the railings either side of me and held tight. All this happened within a fraction of a second and I didn't have a clue what was happening.

As more staff arrived behind me and I let them past it became clear that I'd stopped an officer being pushed down the stairs. Of course, I hadn't known what was going on and it was more self-preservation kicking in, but I didn't protest too much as they commended my quick reaction. What had actually happened was that an inmate was being escorted to the block and had tried to break free by pushing the leading officer down the stairs – and it would have worked if I hadn't been coming up the stairs at exactly that moment. It turned out the inmate had smashed his cell up and refused to leave during a routine search. The PO had tried to talk to him but he'd punched the PO and consequently had to be restrained. He'd seemed to calm down and said he was happy to walk to the block, that there wouldn't be any more problems. Unfortunately, whoever applied the cuffs had done so with the inmate's hands at the front rather than at the back, and when he'd reached the top of the stairs had decided it wasn't all over after all. That fundamental fuckup could have led to serious injuries to a prison officer and it was only blind luck that it didn't.

Once the inmate was safely in the Seg unit, his cell was searched thoroughly. Everyone assumed there must be something particularly 'interesting' in there for him to defend the search so vigorously, but to our surprise, fuck all was found apart from a collection of wank mags, a lot of sugar and four pairs of the cleanest trainers we'd ever seen – all the same brand but two pairs of two different sizes.

In the shit

One evening I was on the threes landing in the cleaning office, having just finished the weekly menu sheets. I stepped out on to the landing and instantly noticed blood – a lot of it. Not the dripping, blotchy kind but the smeary, dragging kind. It looked as if a bloodied corpse had been dragged along the landing. Following the smear marks down the stairs on to the twos, it was then that I heard the alarm being raised. I continued to follow the bloody trail, thinking an officer must have been attacked, and the trail continued down the next flight of stairs on to the ones before disappearing into the wing office.

I entered the office with a degree of trepidation. As I did so, I realised it wasn't an officer who had been injured, as was my initial thought, but an inmate – an especially obnoxious, nasty piece of work. However, his whole demeanour was now changed. Usually this arsewipe would strut his way around the wing with his well-choreographed cat A gangster walk, elbows at least eight inches away from his body as if carrying imaginary rolls of carpet under each arm, shoulders swinging in time to his footsteps, glaring and staring, shaved head and an array of tattoos, all in an attempt to impress or intimidate. Now he was little more than a snivelling, shaking wreck, sporting a very obvious broken arm, a nasty puncture wound on his left upper thigh, lumps, bumps, welts and wounds on his head and face, his nose bleeding and snotty. He was propped up on the only comfy office chair. This had been surreptitiously 'acquired' from the education department and was the chair of choice for any officer settling down into a task for which they'd be sitting down a long time.

The medics arrived along with the cavalry and as the wing was being banged up, the medics did their medical stuff. The rumour was that the other inmates were sick of his hardman act, put the feelers out and found out that he was inside for aggravated burglary. This particular low-life, while robbing a couple of harmless old pensioners, had decided to torture them, tying them to a chair facing each other and then slowly inflicted horrendous pain on each of them in turn, while the other was forced to watch and over a long period of time. As per usual, the battered and bruised inmate was saying fuck all – and fuck all was exactly what each and every other inmate had seen.

We were all keen to get our office with its comfy chair back and a couple of us were waiting as the paramedics left the office.

'He'll be all right, I reckon, but your chair's had it, I'm afraid,' said one medic to our visible shock. 'He'd not only pissed himself but shat himself too.'

Knowing this particular inmate as we did, there was a theory he'd done it deliberately. His parting shot or, should I say, parting shat.

Banged-up electrician

Today we were banging up the wing and were in the process of signing the roll. As the SO was lifting the phone to inform the control room that our 'roll was correct', a cell bell went and as is always the case, it's the landing furthest away: the fours. Fortunately, whoever banged up that particular landing has to go and answer the cell bell, always a bit of a nail-biter because if the inmate on the bell has done something stupid like self-harmed, the officer answering the bell will be knee-deep in paperwork, so it was with some degree of trepidation that this particular officer made the long walk to the fours.

The trouble was the cell bell indicator said it was cell 4-07. This cell was supposed to be empty, confirmed by the roll board having been marked as MT (empty). We watched with bated breath. The officer reached the cell, peeped through the observation flap and then did the unthinkable – unlocked the cell. We started to move up to his landing when he leant over and told us not to bother, there was nothing to worry about. It turned out he had banged up the works electrician, who was fitting a new light in the cell. The sparky was visibly shaken, the officer mortified and we were all in hysterics.

When is a fuckup not a fuckup?

Working in the PWU was something that I had wanted to do since it opened in 1997. The Protected Witness Unit was a super high security unit and held what the press would call 'supergrasses'. The Protected Witness Unit was like C wing and the SSU, and was a national resource. The reason I wanted to work there was for the experience, much the same as my reason for wanting to work on C wing special unit.

I hoped that working in these fascinating, challenging environments would bring out the best in me. By this point, I had become cynical after seeing the way the prison service had treated some quite brilliant staff after the escape, which in my opinion was nothing short of scapegoating to save face. I had given up on my dream of steadily working my way up the ranks and decided I just wanted to be as good a prison officer as I could be. Inmates in the PWU each had a huge price on their head. The security for the SSU was impressive but the PWU was on another level. The inmates located within this unit each had a simple nom de plume while there and consequently were known and named as 'blogs' – i.e. blogs 1, blogs 2, etc. There were drug dealers, armed robbers, corrupt former police officers, a Yardie, an IRA informer and a gangland enforcer. Their ages ranged from early twenties to mid-seventies and their personalities were just as diverse. The monosyllabic thug, the extrovert joker, the introvert thinker, those full of remorse and those who seemed to see their presence there as just part of the game – they were certainly an interesting and challenging group of individuals. When I walked on to the unit for my very first shift, I was being shown around when one of the blogs popped out of the TV room and said, 'Morning, Guv, bet you weren't expecting to see me here!' And he was right because he had previously been a cat A inmate on one of the general wings.

Unlike the main prison, where such a diverse group of inmates could, if needed, avoid each other or at least get away from those inmates they needed to avoid during their working day, exercise, chapel or mealtimes, the PWU was different. It was entirely self-contained and self-sufficient. Once an inmate was in the unit, they never needed to come out. Everything they needed – education, work, visits, a chapel and reception – was on the wing. They had no reason ever to leave the physical confines of that self-contained unit, except maybe to go to court or hospital and that was done with the utmost secrecy. They were taken out undercover and away from prying eyes. It was a major operation and one that was done extremely carefully. There was not a shred of paperwork relating to their real identification, no record of who they really were. It was just as difficult to get on to the actual unit. Hi-tech security gadgets, hand-picked staff and procedures and practices that would make your head spin. No one was allowed to enter the unit, and even governors had to make prior arrangements and be cleared. Everything was on camera and no one approached the unit without being seen. It was then down to a computerised unlocking system operated in a hi-tech control room.

An example of how very tight security was can be explained by an incident that occurred. On this particular day, the vicar had been holding a small service for the three inmates who had wanted to attend. The vicar came in and proceeded to the small multi-faith area used for religious services. He was setting things up when the general alarm went off. This alarm was only activated when things were serious and there was an imminent threat to life, escape in progress or something of that severity. The unit staff were immediately alerted, as were the prison security staff. O1 and the duty governor, who because of the seriously significant nature of the 'Protected Witness Unit', all turned up.

The first to arrive were the black-clad security officers, including one very efficient but very excitable security SO. Unfortunately for him and the boys in black, Barry was in the units control room. Barry was a long-serving, by-the-book, jobsworth kind of officer and rules being rules and procedures being procedures, could not and most definitely would not let anyone in. Then just as the excitable SO was getting even more overly excited by this, O1 arrived on the scene as he was supposed to do, because it's only

O1 that can 'stand down' an incident.[4] However, Barry being a 'rules is rules' officer, he still refused to let anyone into the unit. O1 resorted to ordering him to let O1 on to the unit but still Barry refused. It was a short time later that Victor 2 arrived. V2 is the duty governor, in charge of and the head of the prison, who then asked and then demanded to be let on to the unit but still Barry refused, informing them that the situation had now been resolved.

Now this was like a private refusing a colonel permission to enter the barracks. A furious V2 ordered the prison control room to contact the PWU's principal officer and get them to contact the PWU's control room and instruct Barry to let them in. This was eventually done but only the duty governor was cleared to enter and if and when they were satisfied the 'situation' had been resolved, could they 'stand everyone down'.

Though Barry had done the right thing and had followed the PWU's highly unusual protocol to the letter, he was still given a verbal slapping. It was another case of a no-win situation. Barry was never going to win, he was always going to be in the wrong, no matter what he did so he did the right thing and got a reprimand. With hindsight, if you're going to be in the shit then you might as well do so for doing the right thing! The irony was that although the alarm bell had been pressed, there was no actual alarm bell situation. The vicar thought the alarm bell was the light switch so pressed the bloody thing and was of course totally oblivious to the resulting carnage he had caused.

As no one knew anything about the PWU, it came to

---

4 This means to inform the main prison control room that everything is now sorted and to 'resume normal'.

have a kind of mythical quality in the minds of all the other inmates at Parkhurst. Various teachers would attend the PWU but would have to be rigorously vetted by the Home Office and always collected and escorted to and from the main gate. One particular day I was to escort one of the language teachers back to the main gate after a morning of teaching Spanish. This meant walking through B wing's exercise yard when the inmates were out on their exercise period. The Spanish teacher was a very attractive woman and when I made the return journey back to the unit, one of the inmates came up to me.

'Mr B, you working with the grasses now, who's the bird and why was she in there?' he asked.

'Those grasses get certain perks,' I replied and walked on.

Within a few hours, the rumour flying round the prison was that the grasses had 'brasses' – and the inmates' over-active imaginations had led to the rumour that the prison was now bringing prostitutes in for those in the PWU.[5]

One day I came into work after a four-day weekend and noticed there were padlocks on the inmates' fridge. The inmates in the unit have a small kitchen, a place where they can cook their own food. Food that is purchased via the canteen facilities or some basic foodstuffs were supplied by the main prison and catering department. I asked why padlocks had been put on the fridges and apparently the inmates had noticed that small quantities of foodstuffs had been going missing. This had apparently been going on all week and had caused a degree of friction among them, not quite to the point of fisticuffs but apparently a close-run thing.

---

5   Cockney rhyming slang – brass flute: prostitute.

With each inmate denying 'half-inching' the others' stuff, they decided to set a trap, which soon paid dividends. It was discovered that the night man was the culprit – the OSG (operational support grade) on nights had been helping himself to the odd bit of fruit, chocolate, etc. Not only that, a small amount of money had gone missing from the tea boat box (staff paid £1 a week for teas and coffees), which had also been padlocked. Needless to say, that was the OSG's last night working in the unit.

Today I came into work and saw police cars in the staff car park. Normally, this would not be much cause for concern but today as I walked in, the police walked out with one of the doctors in handcuffs. She had apparently been helping an inmate by supplying, selling or swapping clean urine samples that would clear him and/or others of using drugs. Of course rumours were rife that she did it because of blackmail or even as a result of a sexual relationship.

Catheter

One day, I'd been detailed to 'library escorts', basically collecting inmates from workshops and wings and escorting them to the library. I had just dropped the last of them off on to a wing when the general alarm went off. My radio sprang to life: 'alarm bell remand unit, alarm bell remand unit'. Being quite close, I legged it to the remand wing and on entering, was immediately directed by one of the cleaners (who in days gone by would be called a 'trusty' or 'red band') to one of the cells. I got to the cell door just in time to see two officers attempting to restrain an inmate.

Apparently, this inmate had been going to have his cell searched but he'd had other ideas, got into an argument, started shouting the odds before making the mistake of taking a swing at one of the officers. It had connected, smacking the officer on the side of the head. It was then that the officers hit the bell and attempted to restrain the inmate. They had just about got him to the floor when I arrived. Lying on his stomach, the officers were attempting to control his arms. The inmate was still very much in fighting mode, wriggling, kicking, spitting and snarling. I immediately went for his legs to stop the kicking, eventually getting them under control by putting them in a 'figure of four'.[6]

All this had happened in a very short space of time and the other staff were now just arriving. The PO asked what had happened and the two other officers explained that they were about to search the cell when the inmate kicked off. This, it was decided, implied that there was something not only worth hiding, but worth fighting for. It was at this point that I realised I might just have found the thing he was trying so desperately to hide. There was, I noticed, something hidden beneath his left trouser leg – a soft, squidgy package on the side of his leg between knee and ankle. I informed the PO that I thought I'd found something, gloating in my super-duper searching skill set.

Slowly, and with all the skill of a well-practised magician, I rolled up his trouser leg ready to reveal what was so obviously an illicit item, the item that had caused all the commotion, only to reveal a urinary collection bag. It turned out the inmate had been fitted with a catheter

---

6 An officially approved position for controlling the legs during a C&R incident.

owing to an ongoing medical condition and I had now revealed to the world that he was suffering incontinence. Nothing was ever found in his cell and the explanation for his violent reaction to being searched was never revealed.

Cell clearance

Today on D wing, another officer and I were tasked with doing a cell clearance. The previous occupant of this particular cell had recently been removed to the Seg unit under restraint. He had been removed from the wing by Security owing to 'information received', which usually meant that somebody had for whatever reason wanted him off the wing and had surreptitiously put a note in the wing mailbox stating this inmate was going to assault staff, had hidden drugs or was planning an escape – anything that would warrant him being lifted (removed from the wing to the block) or ghosted (removed and transferred to another prison).

This particular inmate was not normally a problem to staff, an armed robber and a bit of a Walter Mitty but not a discipline problem – until that was when the officers went in to lift him. It was then that he got a bit gobby, threatened to fight and started kicking things and throwing a massive tantrum.

Most of the time when someone is removed from the wing, either lifted or ghosted, it's done first thing in the morning. Done before inmates are awake. Inmates, by and large, are not stupid and if they know that the chances are they will be lifted, the sensible, longer-serving ones will have already been prepared, packed their 'essential items' themselves and accepted their fate. They just get escorted off the wing and then the other inmates only find out that so-and-so is missing when we don't unlock his cell. Occasionally they won't go quietly and this particular inmate had chosen to do so – he refused to go without a fight (this usually means one of two things: he has something to hide or he's been stitched up). Fortunately, he was by nature not a fighter but on this occasion he was more boisterous, very angry and very loud. He struggled, put on a bit of a show and created a scene, albeit a loud noisy scene – loud enough to wake most of the wing, who were always pissed off when woken and even more pissed off when one of their own was being lifted. Doors were being kicked and banged, shouts of 'leave him alone, you cunts', the standard warning call of 'fucking burglars on the wing'.

Annoying as it was, the noise was never usually a problem – until that is, it was time to unlock. It was then that you needed to be switched on and aware of each other.

Missing

If an inmate is seriously injured and the Healthcare Centre can't provide care, they are taken to a local hospital. I was working what's called an 'M shift' one day when a fight broke out on another wing and an inmate was badly injured.[7] He was so badly hurt he needed to be sent out for treatment. It was 4 p.m. and I was looking forward to heading home soon, but the PO asked if I would be able to accompany the inmate to hospital and stay with him until the night shift arrived. Being keen to impress and

---

7 Basically, a morning and afternoon shift which is supposed to be the sort of hours most people would think of as a working day.

knowing that my wife was on the mainland (or the North Island, as locals call it) visiting her family, I said that I would be able to extend. Another officer and I took him to the local hospital, where they said that owing to a rather nasty head injury, he'd have to be in overnight. We hung about until about 8.30 p.m. when the night staff arrived, then I changed into my cycling gear and rode home.

I was woken up by my wife staring down at me with a mixture of relief and anger. I was doubly confused as she wasn't due back until the following day. My first thought was that I hadn't done the washing-up.

'Where the bloody hell have you been?' she said.

'Erm, here,' I said.

It became clear that she had called me at home the previous evening and not getting an answer, had worried so she called the prison to check on me and was informed that I was on an M shift and my keys were in the key safe, so I'd already left prison at 5.30 at the end of my shift. She made a couple of calls, including one to the hospital where I was accompanying the inmate, to see if a cyclist had been hit by a car and brought in.[8] She called the house again to no answer so she drove the nearly 200 miles south, caught the very last ferry and rushed home, worrying all the time that I was lying unconscious in a ditch somewhere.

I had to explain what exactly had happened and that I was indeed at the hospital but with an inmate. Fortunately, she was now more relieved than angry. I vowed there and then never to volunteer again!

---

8 This was the mid-nineties, so neither of us had a mobile phone.

CHAPTER 7

Can't Get the Staff

A VIP visit to the prison was always accompanied by frenetic activity. Everything received an extra dose of spit and polish and everyone put their best foot forward. Shortly before I joined, Her Royal Highness Princess Anne was visiting and at one point she was introduced to some of the Seg unit officers. They were all standing in a line, standing to attention in their best, freshly pressed uniforms. Her Royal Highness was doing the regal and serene procession down the line – 'Hello, what's your name, how are you, how long have you worked in the service?', that type of thing. Things were proceeding smoothly until she got to Norm.

Princess Anne: 'Hello, how are you?'

Norm: 'Well, actually, I've been having a lot of trouble sleeping due to this ongoing back problem.' At which point he began lifting his shirt up to show her.

Princess Anne: 'Oh dear.'

As the other officers tried desperately to keep a straight face, Norm was utterly oblivious to the chaos he'd caused. Princess Anne continued her visit and finished the day having seen a state-of-the-art Seg unit and rather a lot of Norm's poorly back.

Prison officers, it would be fair to say, are as different to each other as the inmates are. Different religions, backgrounds, sexual orientations, ex-greengrocers and green jackets, from the gruff army sergeant major on parade to the softly spoken Sunday school teacher, the academically gifted and the academically challenged, former professional footballers and amateur boxers, accountants and cartoonists, those who had been majors and those who had been miners. A lot were, it would be fair to say, comfortable on a wing, not overly impressed or fazed by the violence around them.

Like inmates, officers earned respect from their peers. Some were skilful at reading people and situations, picking up on the smallest of nuances, spotting flaws in the system and knowing how to take advantage of any given situation. The more experienced officer, like the old school con, knew the rules and often they had some sort of mutual understanding. But some of them didn't know their arse from their elbow. One colleague, who developed a habit for forgetting to lock up inmates, was already on shaky ground because he was entirely missing that necessary air of authority. However, he did make up for it by possessing a distinctive and all-pervasive unpleasant body aroma – he was the only officer I ever knew who was actually ordered by a SO to shower and collect a fresh shirt from stores. He was absolutely clueless and didn't seem to be able to retain any sort of information, no matter how serious. To this day, he probably thinks his nickname – 'The Hummer' – was because he hummed the odd tune or two.

Norm with the poorly back was an interesting character: strong as an ox and daft as a brush. He was utterly fearless but not academically gifted, the sort of bloke who could lift a ton but would have trouble spelling it. Norm was an amateur mechanic who loved nothing more than tinkering with cars. One day, a colleague arrived late to work, complaining that their pushbike was on its last legs and he needed to get it repaired or he would have to bite the bullet and buy a new one. Norm, being ever helpful, assured him there was no need and that he'd be happy to fix it free of charge. He collected the bike, took it home and over the next few days proceeded to take every bit of it apart, cleaning and labelling every single piece. But when it came to putting it back together, he realised there was a flaw in his plan as he had absolutely no idea how to put it back together again. The bemused officer ended up being given half a dozen or so cardboard boxes full of bike bits and Norm shaking his head, saying, 'I don't know what's the matter with the fucking thing, you'll have to buy a new one.'

Prison officers also come in all shapes and sizes, from big and slightly slow to small and very fast . . .

Mighty Mouse

One week I was working a week of nights in the Emergency Control Room (ECR). In those days, there were four officers and one senior officer who was in overall charge. One officer went down and worked in the gate while three officers and the SO remained in the control room, watching the many CCTV cameras, monitoring and controlling all communication and any movement inside and outside the prison grounds. It was one of those postings where for 80 per cent of the time you did a whole lot of not very much, but the remaining 20 per cent would be a flurry of activity and this flurry required each individual to follow a well-rehearsed set of procedures. Basically, if you were busy, you were busy because there was some sort of emergency.

This was my first set of nights in the ECR so I was slowly learning, reading about procedures, asking questions and being shown how and when to do certain things. The SO in the control room, a hyperactive, multitasking, fast-talking individual who appeared to be suffering from a rather bad case of horrendous haemorrhoids, evidenced by the fact he never actually sat down or stood still, had earned the nickname Mighty Mouse. A nervous ball of hyperactivity, he flitted from one place to another, looking over your shoulder, micro-managing and double-checking everything. This in turn transmitted itself to the other staff until everyone on the team was a bundle of nerves, ready to jump at everything. It got so bad that one shift, his colleagues 'accidentally' locked him in the toilet for twenty minutes. While they tried desperately to fix the 'faulty' lock, they had a brew and a breather. This particular night, Mighty was still in full flow at 2.30 a.m. When he disappeared to make himself something to eat, one of the other officers, who was a bit of an artist, decided to put his artistic skills to good use. Grabbing a dry wipe marker pen, he made his way over to one of the black and white monitors for a camera that was pointing to one of the internal wall sections. He very quickly drew a ladder leaning against that particular wall, which looked impressively real.

Mighty returned eating a Pot Noodle and as predicted, the first thing he did was scan the screens. We saw him go rigid as he spotted what he thought was a fully-blown escape and leapt into action, throwing his Pot Noodle in the bin, calling orders and reaching for the phone in one fluid movement. Bear in mind that this was a man who made choosing a biscuit to go with his brew a high-stress military manoeuvre. By this point, half the staff were laughing hysterically and he couldn't understand why no one was leaping into action until the artist calmly walked over and wiped the screen clean. Mighty was left to mutter 'You're a bunch of absolute cunts' to himself darkly as he retrieved his Pot Noodle from the bin.

Rules are rules

James was a lovely fella, quietly spoken and incredibly intelligent. One of those extremely clever, academically bright individuals who was as thick as fuck. But the real trouble was that James didn't seem to apply common sense where the inmates were concerned. Any rule, however minor, was treated with the same seriousness. Balls the size of coconuts, he wouldn't stand for any nonsense, whoever the inmate was. For example, one day we were both walking up towards the fours landing and James was just ahead of me when he noticed that a cell card had been ripped and bent.[1] For some reason, James really hated anyone tampering with cell cards. It was a pain and definitely not permitted by the rules, but of course inmates being inmates, they quickly realised that to do so would massively wind him up so they did it.

James went storming into the cell and threatened to place the inmate on report for wilful damage to prison property. I noticed that voices were slowly being raised so I popped my head in and immediately spotted a smouldering sheet and a rapidly developing and rather nasty-looking welt developing just below one inmate's eye, whose T-shirt had also been ripped. Clearly, we were in the middle of some sort of threat or warning and the inmate had been

---

1 Every inmate had a cell card outside their cell on the wall with key information on it: name, sentence, religion, etc.

slapped about a bit, his sheet set on fire. However, James in his myopic fury could only see the damaged cell card.

Another time I had been sent to collect an inmate who had had a blazing row with his wife during a visit and I had to return him to the wing. His wife had apparently told him in no uncertain terms that she wanted an immediate divorce then it had all kicked off with raised voices, swearing and tears, and threatened to get out of hand. The other inmates who were trying to have an all-too-precious moment with friends and/or family were rudely disrupted.

This particular inmate had a famously short fuse coupled with a violent temper and the fact that he was no fan of screws at the best of times meant that it could only end in chaos. So, after hearing his wife wanted a divorce and knowing he'd already kicked off once about having to be searched, I could tell he was on a hair trigger and we walked in silence. Then we saw James, who immediately came over and started loudly telling the inmate he needed to pull his trousers up. Like many inmates, his rather strange choice was to have his trousers hanging halfway down his legs, with the waistband below his arse cheeks, leaving a pair of rather colourful boxers on full display. I tried to signal silently with my eyes that this really wasn't the best time but I could see that James had started to wind himself up for a lecture. Grabbing his arm, I said, 'I'll sort it, James.' As we carried on walking, I felt the inmate unclench every muscle in his body as my colleague went on his way, oblivious to how close to things going very pear-shaped we'd come.

As I say, a very bright bloke in many ways – just not many ways that were useful as a prison officer. The following day, we had to delay unlocking the wing because James wasn't on duty yet and this meant that we were below MSL.[2] James had contacted the gate to let them know he was going to be a little bit late. The gate then informed the principal officer, O1, who then had to find another member of staff to give us a hand to unlock and stay on the wing until James arrived. The strange thing was that James had 'contacted the gate', not by phone but in person. He had driven the nearly five miles from his house to the prison to tell them he would be late before driving back off to do whatever he had to do that was going to make him late.

Bang yourself up

I was talking to an officer on the landing one day when an inmate called Jock approached us. He was a morose, rather depressing individual. A Scotsman who had apparently once been a big-time drinker, he now had a face like a tenderised steak. He'd clearly had a tough, violent street life. He spoke quietly, the words were soft and gentle and chosen wisely; a soft Scottish lilt, not the hard, aggressive Glaswegian accent that might be expected. Jock also had an unfortunate personal hygiene problem and during the summer this was beyond compare – he was one of the few individuals you could smell before you saw him; you could quite literally smell him before he entered the room. But I'd never known him to be violent or show aggression.

As Jock and his unpleasant odour approached, my fellow officer and I were both wondering why he was approaching us. It was very out of character and what was even weirder,

---

2   Minimum staffing levels – basically not enough staff to unlock the wing.

he seemed to be holding a pair of sunglasses and what appeared to be a ladies' purse. The confusion was resolved when he finally handed my colleague the purse, a set of car keys and the sunglasses. He explained that the female officer had left them over there, pointing to the TV room. Jock went on to explain that she had been in the TV room, watching TV with a couple of the inmates and had got up to apparently use the loo but left behind her glasses, car keys and purse containing cash, credit cards, a photo and her address. Any officer with an ounce of common sense never ever brings personal items into a prison and certainly not on to a wing.

We worked out that the officer he meant was one who had only been in the prison service for a little less than a year but had already made an impressive name for herself. She had 'banged herself up' more than any other officer and held that record for the rest of the time I was in the service. 'Shooting the bolt' is one of the most fundamental basic things an officer does when entering a cell and becomes habit, like flushing the toilet or cleaning your teeth. Because if you don't shoot the bolt, the door is going to shut, accidentally or deliberately. Of course inmates find it absolutely hilarious to 'bang up' an officer by slamming the cell door with them inside. It's then impossible for you to get out and you have to call for assistance.

The strange thing was that this particular officer had made it clear to anyone who would listen that her university education would ensure that she was on a fast track to governor. This delusion would have been fine but the scary thing was her incompetence not only put her at risk but other officers too. A prime example of this was when she went missing. No one, but no one, knew where she was. Worryingly, she had a radio and had even 'joined the net' because she was supposed to be in a workshop, she was late and consequently every available prison officer, physical education instructor (PEI), works officers and education staff was asked if they knew her whereabouts. There were repeated calls to her radio call sign but still, there was nothing. She was officially reported as missing and all available staff were instructed to search everywhere, whereupon she was eventually found in an inmate's cell.

When the senior officer told her that the whole prison had been brought to a standstill and everyone was looking for her, her reply was, 'Why? I was just talking to Danny, he's had some bad news!' The SO asked why she hadn't answered her radio and her rather curt reply was, 'Because it kept going off and I was trying to talk to Danny.' Her dismissive attitude was a terrible mix of high-handed and naive and she had put herself and her colleagues in danger. The worrying thing was she couldn't see it and most certainly wouldn't accept it. She was subsequently told to go and see the wing governor, which didn't end well as she argued her case forcibly and wouldn't listen then stormed out of the office. Needless to say, she didn't remain as an officer for long.

She became a governor.

A rose by any other name . . .

One day I was detailed to work in the Healthcare Centre (HCC) as the runner. Normally two officers work there: one does the admin, the other does the running. The officer I was working with was fairly new, just a few weeks into the job. I hadn't actually worked with him before but had seen him around the place and knew his nickname was Stan. He had already made an impression on his wing for not being the sharpest tool in the box. It was generally thought that he was a little bit slow to grasp things and not blessed with a great deal of common sense. He did, however, somehow seem to have a bulletproof confidence that I wished I'd been blessed with when I started. He was the perfect combination of someone who fucks everything up but never needs anything explained to them.

Once the HCC staff were ready, we started getting the inmates in for 'treatments'. They came and collected their prescribed medication or saw the doctor, dentist, psychologist, chiropodist, yoga practitioner and the CARATs worker, as we made our way down the list.[3] Some inmates arrived straight from the wings but many had to be collected from various workshops, wings, the gym, library, etc. and that was the runner's job. I had been at it for a couple of hours when Stan asked me to collect an inmate called Morgan from one of the workshops so I made my way over and informed the instructor that I would be taking Morgan to Healthcare as he had an appointment. Unfortunately, he didn't have anyone called Morgan – there was no one of that name on his list of 'employees'.

Just then an inmate approached and said, 'Guv, I've got to be in Healthcare in five minutes.' I asked his name. 'Maughan,' he replied. I checked my list and told him he was not on the list. I checked his ID card and again confirmed that he was not on the list. At this point, as some inmates tend to do, he hit the roof, calling me a liar and

---

3 Counselling, Assessment, Referral, Advice and Throughcare – basically the drug and alcohol treatment counsellors.

accusing the wing of playing mind games and informing me that I really didn't know who I was dealing with, he wasn't a fucking pushover, you'd fucking see, blah blah and bloody blah. Once this aggressive tirade had died down, I called his wing, explaining that he was to return to the wing as he was agitated and not safe to remain in the workshop, and they sent someone over to collect him. I was thinking gloomily about the paperwork that would result from the nicking I'd have to give him.

Returning to the HCC, I let Stan know what had happened: there was no Morgan but there was now a pissed-off Maughan. It was only then that he realised Morgan and Maughan were one and the same. He had the list in front of him and showed me the name Maughan.

'Look,' he said, 'Morgan, right there.' That's not how you pronounce Morgan, it's pronounced MORN!

He absolutely wouldn't have it that he'd made a mistake. I told him he needed to phone the wing, get Maughan to Healthcare and explain the mix-up. My annoyance at his confident cockiness was only relieved by the fact I wouldn't have to nick Maughan after all.

About an hour later, we were doing treatments – this is when each wing sends any inmates that have been prescribed prescriptions that need collecting and/or administering. This could be pain relief, heart medication, athletes' foot fungal cream, haemorrhoid treatment or methadone. They would collect these from a small serving hatch or go into the Healthcare admin room, where it would be administered and monitored. Because medication is often a potential flashpoint, one officer stays by the hatch and the other stays in the admin area. It's a pain-in-the-arse job that happens three times a day. The amount of pills, creams, lotions and potions dispensed at these times is frightening – the NHS actually employs an individual whose sole aim in life is to collect and deliver transit boxes full of prescribed meds from the pharmacy to the Healthcare and then on to to the prisoners. I was always staggered by the quantity of prescribed medication that some inmates were collecting: boxes of pills, lotions, potions, creams and suppositories, plasters, medicated shampoo, E45 cream, lozenges, Anusol and hand cream. It is fortunate indeed that the inmates, unlike much of the general population, don't need to pay for their prescriptions.[4]

Mo

Mo was a lovely fella – friendly, keen and so pleased to finally be a prison officer as it was a job he had wanted to do for some time. He was a practising Muslim and a couple of times a shift, resplendent in his kufi skull cap, he would nip off for prayers. Keen as mustard, he was willing to get stuck in and learn the ropes. With his disarming smile and pleasant demeanour he was soon one of the team, however he was not blessed with great common sense and only ever saw the very best in people, a distinct disadvantage when dealing with the very worst of people.

One day we had a 'stand still roll check' – this is where every inmate on every landing on every wing is counted at the same time. Each landing hands their total number

---

4   The same goes for the TV licence. While for the general population it is a criminal offence not to pay for a TV licence, the convicted felon doesn't have to pay and at least 98 per cent of prisoners have a television in their cell.

of inmates to the officer responsible for the wing roll, who is known as the 'collator'. There's always a bit of friendly competition as no wing ever wants to be the last to put their roll in. Unfortunately, this time the numbers for our wing didn't add up so we then did a recount with each officer counting a different landing than the one he had originally banged up and counted. But again, the numbers didn't tally.

Usually when I did a landing roll check I had a piece of paper and just marked each empty cell with MT (empty). On the third count I suggested each of us do the same and it quickly became apparent that cell 3-03 was empty and shouldn't have been − the inmate who occupied that cell should have been on the wing and banged up. The now-panicking collator confirmed that he had not left the wing and therefore should have indeed been on the wing and behind his door. We were now the only wing that hadn't been able to give the control room a 'wing roll', so the whole prison was waiting for us. If we couldn't account for each of our inmates the shit would hit the fan and the whole prison would go into full lockdown, with all gates frozen and no one going in or out.

It was at this moment that Mo said very matter-of-factly that he had let the inmate out of the wing earlier so he could do his cleaning job. Mo was sent to collect the 'missing' inmate and bang him up. Then and only then could we confirm that the wing roll was correct. When asked why he had not told the collator that he had let an inmate off the wing, he replied, 'Cos he was only in the corridor.' As I say, Mo was a lovely fella but he quickly realised that the job was not for him, he was just too nice.

He left the service a few months later.

Worzel

Worzel was an officer who got his nickname owing to his permanently dishevelled appearance, which led some people to say he looked like the scarecrow Worzel Gummidge. He was one of those unfortunate individuals who was always scruffy and always grubby. Without any problem whatsoever, he could wear the same white shirt for days at a time and once wore the same shirt for five days straight. Staff knew this for a fact because they were actually running a book on how long he would wear a particular shirt. Many a Mars bar was won or lost betting on his fashion habits. He was also one of those people who you could tell what they'd had for breakfast every day that week. Beans, egg, tea stains and other, more mysterious marks adorned his uniform. This was one of the ways that you knew who had won the bet. If a particularly memorable jumper stain had disappeared one morning, you had a winner! Though pretty slovenly, he was a very likeable officer, good at his job apart from his uniform and timekeeping. Late on duty at least twice a week, he didn't wear a watch and when it was suggested he might buy one, he said he wasn't going to because he didn't need one.

One day Worzel was late again, keeping everyone waiting and delaying the unlocking of the wing. When he finally did arrive, rather than apologise and get up on to the landing ASAP, he sauntered off into the tea room to make a brew. Unfortunately, the principal officer was also waiting for him and told him in terms of the utmost clarity that he should cease the preparation of a hot drink and immediately proceed with all haste to his landing. Basically, fuck off and get on to the landing! Once he'd done the unlock, he was then summoned to the PO's office. This was a bit like being summoned to the headmaster's office and the only reason for it would usually be for a rollocking to be delivered. Sure enough, there was the sound of raised voices and though the nearest officers as is their wont tried to listen, they couldn't quite make out what was being said. After several minutes Worzel appeared, seemingly totally relaxed, and started making a brew.

'Blimey, who's upset the PO?' he said, squeezing a teabag against the side of his mug.

We just stared at him. To be so oblivious was, we decided, a kind of superpower.

Whatever the PO had said to him, it looked like it had worked as Worzel was on time for his next three shifts. Perhaps there had been a brave new dawn. However, on the fourth shift, he was late. He arrived at the gate late and was told to hurry his arse up so he started running on to the wing. One of the physical education instructors saw Worzel running and ran after him.[5] Then one of the hospital officers saw both of them running and fell in behind them. Worzel's route took him past the training classroom, where another two officers joined, and the fire officer's office. They heard the sound of running, saw five staff pelting it towards the wing and assumed something big must be kicking off, so sprinted after them all. After all, that was the only time you'd ever see that many members of staff running in a prison. At which point, Worzel had to turn around sheepishly and explain there was no alarm bell, he was just a bit late.

---

5 We never found out why he started running. Maybe PEIs are like dogs and cars.

In spite of his timekeeping, Worzel was a popular member of the team because he was good at so many other parts of the job. The worst was when you had a colleague who was very good at looking good at the job but was actually a useless team member.

I was returning from the gym one day after having dropped off half a dozen cat A books when the radio sprang to life: 'Alarm bell delta, alarm bell delta, code red'. This almost always meant someone was bleeding, either through self-harm or a fight, but there was always the thought at the back of your mind that it might be a colleague. Unfortunately, I had fallen in behind an experienced but rather unfit officer on the way. I knew he was experienced because he had stopped to put his cap on before he set off – the older, more experienced officers came from a generation where prison officers had certain standards of uniform. I could also tell he was unfit, because he threw his half-smoked fag away as we got to the wing and this was followed by a honked-up greenie fired with such precision, it hit his discarded fag butt.

Fortunately for us the gate to the wing was being held open by a massive lump of an officer, who directed us to the three landing. I, of course, decided that experience and bulk were better off in front of me rather than behind, so didn't even try to pass the large, unfit bloke in front. Just as we reached the twos, a rather bruised and battered inmate surrounded by staff came towards us. The inmate I noticed was now rapidly turning several shades of an interesting colour. When interviewed in the HCC, it turned out he hadn't been watching where he was going and had tripped over his own two feet, catching his head on his cell table as he went down.[6] Rumour had it the real story was that he'd foolishly tried a bit of pad thievery, been caught and given a very physical warning. On our way back from the wing, once things had been 'stood down', I fell into step next to the experienced officer.

'Who was the big unit holding the gates open for us?'

'Ah yes,' he replied. 'That rather impressive specimen would be Rucksack.'

'Rucksack?' I said. 'Why do they call him that?'

'Because he has to be carried on every shift.'

Every now and then you met officers like that, who talked a very good game and looked the part but when it came down to it, were fucking useless.

One evening, another officer and I were leaning over the railings, watching the inmates on association, when all of a sudden, our attention was drawn to a cell on the ones, where it became clear there was definitely something happening so we made our way down and went straight to the cell. Lo and behold, two inmates were beating the shit out of each other. There was already a reasonable amount of claret. We dived in, split them up and were met with a verbal onslaught of threats – fucks were being thrown around like confetti. Both of us had our hands full, holding them back from tearing lumps out of each other, and weren't able to raise the alarm.

Luckily the noise was such that the senior officer came out and could be seen at the gate watching us as we held the inmates apart. He was, I noticed, wearing a green first aider badge so I assumed that what would happen

---

6   Those dodgy Victorian building practices again!

would be that he would raise the alarm, then come in, help us restrain them and then perhaps offer some sort of medical intervention. Instead, he just stood there, frozen. He didn't move towards us or hit the alarm, just stood there. Fortunately, it was only a few seconds later that another officer arrived, raised the alarm and came to lend us a hand. Once more reinforcements arrived, we managed to get one inmate banged up and the other taken to the HCC, but the SO was nowhere to be seen. I'll never know what had happened but he was off work for quite a while and eventually left the service.

Drop him!

Sometimes though you just had to admire the way an officer worked. One evening early on, I saw an impressive PO at work. One that Fulton Mackay's Mr Mackay in the BBC sitcom *Porridge* could have been based on: a no-nonsense, fearless Welshman. The sort of PO that the inmates hated but respected and the staff respected and would follow into any shitty situation. He was one of those leaders that lead you into the shit rather than send you into it.

That particular evening an inmate came into the office who was a particularly nasty piece of work. He hated screws, his fellow inmates and authority and loved nothing more than having a bit of a tear-up. He and this officer could have been designed to wind each other up. The inmate told us – and it was very much a telling, not an asking – that he needed to make a phone call. We let him know that unfortunately the list was full but he insisted: he'd had some bad news and needed to 'speak to his people'. There are some occasions when it's possible to bend rules if the situation demands it, but this wasn't going to be one of them. The principal officer walked in just as this was being explained to him, that the list was full and he wasn't going to be able to jump the queue. He cheerfully added his opinion, telling the inmate that he wasn't going to be using the phone. The inmate raised his voice but the principal officer raised a smile whereupon the inmate raised his fist and the principal officer raised the alarm, along with instructions to the two nearest officers to 'drop him'. Within a split second, the inmate was on the floor and in wrist locks, being escorted to the Seg unit for threatening behaviour.

Street smarts

Sometimes you just had to hold your hands up to some of the senior officers and their wily ways. When I first arrived at Parkhurst from training college, half the prison was being refurbished and part of the refurbishment was a new Seg unit. Once that was finished, the tricky process began of moving the old Seg unit inmates into the new one. When this was done, the two new wings – A and D – were to be filled with B and M wing inmates – this had to be done as those wings, including the old Seg, were then going to be gutted and refurbished. All the old wooden flooring and wooden cell doors were being replaced and modernised. Every single cell in Parkhurst would then be of a cat A standard, a super secure structure.[7]

Shortly after the new Seg unit was filled and occupied,

---

7   Having prisoners escape and losing cat A status was, of course, not part of the plan.

it was time to relocate both B and M wings. Most of M wing would occupy A wing and most of the B wing inmates would occupy D wing. The wing management had sorted out the staffing levels, and who was to work where (I was to be posted to D wing). Once this was done, it was time to decide where each of the inmates would be located. The security PO at the time was an experienced wily old screw. He played what, at the time, seemed a controversial hand – he went and had a word with the Georgious, a trio of brothers who were the unofficial leaders of the wing hier-archy and part of a criminal organisation heavily involved with armed robbery, racketeering, and drug dealing and trafficking. They had a powerful following on the wing but had, as you might expect, never actually raised their heads above the prison parapet (instead getting others to do that on their behalf). They had on a couple of occasions been savvy enough to use that clout to score brownie points: once when an inmate had become troublesome and needed a quiet word to keep in line and a couple of times when a large metal serving spoon had gone missing. As I'm sure you'll realise by now, a large metal spoon can be crafted into an extremely dangerous weapon in prison. Realising that they didn't want the hassle of a full wing spin any more than we did,[8] lo and behold, the spoon was 'found' and everyone could get on as usual.

Spotting a unique opportunity, the PO decided to have an informal chat with the Georgious and ask for their help in deciding who should go where in the new D wing, seeing as they knew far better than any of us the state of the relationships between inmates on their wing. He brought

---

8 Where staff do a full search of the whole wing.

a list of the inmates and was in the middle of explaining that some of the cells looked out over the forest directly behind the prison and would, in effect, come with a view when he was called away to take an urgent phone call. He asked the Georgious if they were happy to carry on putting their suggestions down and he'd pop back later and they could all carry on.

Thinking this was too good an opportunity to pass up, the Georgious duly made up a list of who should go where. The brothers got the best cells, then their good friends and associates got the next and on down through the floors in order of how nice a room the Georgious thought their fellow inmates should get. They thought they were making a list of which prisoners should go where, whereas in fact they were writing a map of the entire wing pecking order, with the great and the good up in the penthouse on the fours, all the way down to the dregs and the dross on the ones.

Turning the other cheek

I was once told about an officer at another prison who had been placed under investigation for apparently beating the shit out of a prisoner. This was and indeed is a very serious allegation. However, this particular allegation was made all the more credible by the fact that the assault was witnessed not by another inmate but by the prison chaplain. Apparently, the vicar was on the wing when he heard an almighty (sorry!) commotion and then looking up towards the twos landing from where the sound emanated, he heard an officer quite clearly and unmistakably say, 'What the fuck did you do that for? You fucking idiot!' This was then followed by the officer dragging the 'fucking idiot' out from a cell. The inmate appeared to be limp, possibly semi-conscious. The officer then dropped him, bent over him and proceeded to pummel him with his fists. The vicar left the wing and contacted the governor, informing him of what he had just had the misfortune to witness.

However, what actually happened and what the vicar actually saw were two entirely different things. An inmate, some moments before, had approached an officer (the accused) and said that Miller was going to 'top himself'. Knowing Miller of old, the officer then went and checked on him. As he approached, Miller set fire to his shirt. The officer then said, 'What the fuck did you do that for? You fucking idiot!', grabbed the now-panicking inmate, threw him to the floor and desperately patted out the now-ignited shirt with his bare hands, suffering slight blistering and a couple of small burns. Help was summoned and both Miller and his rescuer were taken to the HCC. The officer was later thanked by the inmate and still later investigated by the governors. Ironically though, the inmate later apologised to the officer, but the vicar never did apologise, resolutely sticking to the fact that he saw the officer beating an inmate.

As was famously said, you often see more of the people you work with than your own family or loved ones. There is a delicate balance when you work in a team in as high stakes an environment as a prison. A good colleague can brighten up a work day, a bad one can put your life in danger. There is also a fine balance between the young staff, who are learning on the job, and the more experienced officers, who are the keepers of the prison staff culture. I witnessed this at first hand when, after twenty years working at Parkhurst, I moved the short distance to the neighbouring Albany prison.

CHAPTER 8

Albany

Parkhurst and Albany were next-door neighbours and quite literally a stone's throw away from each other. However, this close physical proximity didn't stop the prisons from being worlds apart. There had originally been three prisons on the Isle of Wight – Parkhurst, Albany and Camp Hill. The prisoners held in each were vastly different, which meant they had vastly different working practices. These somewhat bespoke local working practices had over a period of time developed to ensure the smoothest possible running of each uniquely different prison: each of the prisons had very different inmates, with very different needs and very different problems, so the ways the staff had of dealing with each were, of course, different. Basically, there was the Parkhurst way, the Albany way and the Camp Hill way.

Camp Hill was built in 1912 using prisoner labour from Parkhurst and up until 2013 when it was closed, it was a category C prison. Albany was a relatively new prison, built in 1967 and designed as a category C training prison. A short time after its opening, it was upgraded to a cat B and then just three years after opening in 1970, it was decided to upgrade the prison to the high-security cat A dispersal prison. Even to the layman this disgraceful level of indecision and woeful incompetence was worrying.

The infrastructure and fabric of the prison building were designed for cat C use, but it was then changed to cat B and then inexplicably, the purpose-built cat C prison became a high-security cat A, all within a thirty-six-month period. The staff would not have known their arse from their elbow, and regime changes and the very type of inmate would have been confusing and dangerous. This unfortunately proved to be the case with Albany later achieving the unenviable reputation as the 'most violent dispersal prison in the country'. Unrest was commonplace, culminating in a rooftop demonstration in May 1983 after a week's worth of trouble, with numerous fires, fights and riots. In 1990, a firebomb exploded in A wing's television room. Fortunately the explosion occurred when all the inmates were in their cells, however it was soon discovered that this was more through good luck than by design as the improvised bomb's fuse was faulty and though intended to explode when the television room was full, it failed and the lucky inmates were locked up and behind their cell doors. Another stroke of good fortune was that the prison officers had not left the prison. Five minutes later and the staff would have left the prison, instead seconds after the explosion they raced back to 'rescue' the inmates by evacuating the wing. Had they not been in the prison the explosion would have caused any number of casualties. Over the years there developed a friendly inter-prison rivalry, not to mention a very unofficial hierarchy which, according to Parkhurst staff: Parkhurst was on top, Albany next, followed by Camp Hill (I'm sure each saw themselves as number one!).

Before I went to work there, my only experience of Albany was meeting some officers who, when HMP Albany was taken out of the dispersal system, had been deployed to work at Parkhurst. The different approach to the same job was a bit of an eye-opener for someone like me, who had only ever worked in one prison, i.e. HMP Parkhurst. Parkhurst was indeed lucky that some of the Albany prison officers were hugely experienced, extremely professional and enthusiastic, however others were less so.

The inmates in Parkhurst were a very different type to those in Albany and they certainly didn't like change. For them the plethora of new faces was something else to be exploited. A couple of the less robust Albany officers were apprehensive, to say the least, about working on a Parkhurst landing. The trouble was inmates being inmates, they soon realised it. As any prison officer knows only too well, you have to front it out as best you can; you can't show any weakness or fear because if you do, your life becomes a lot harder and a lot more miserable. If the inmates can intimidate you into making a mistake, then they can use that mistake as leverage to blackmail you – potentially getting you to seriously break the rules. Then they've got you properly.

One rather reluctant Albany officer was doing his first shift on a wing at Parkhurst and came across a couple of blocked spyholes. This blocking of spyholes was the norm and was usually resolved pretty quickly with a quick kick of the door accompanied by a 'You in there?' The reply was usually along the lines of 'Fuck off, Guv, I'm having a crap/wank/breakdown', etc. Either way, you would then tell them in no uncertain terms to unblock the spyhole by the time you got back. The only time it ever really became a problem was when you didn't get an answer, then you stood your ground, banged on the door until you got one and if not, you got another couple of officers, informed the control room that you were about to 'open one up' and then and only then did you check on the cell's occupier. If he didn't answer because he was half-dead, you got the medics – and if he didn't answer because he was an arsehole who thought it funny, you nicked him.

The Albany officer came across two such blocked spyholes, knocked on the doors of each cell and got no answer and then rather bizarrely, he left the landing rather than confirm what the status of the inmate was. He went to the senior officer and informed him that there were a couple of blocked spyholes. Later, when he was no longer at Parkhurst, he would say the SO told him to sign for the roll anyway. This would, of course, have been an absolute no-no – you never ever sign to say inmates are where they should be unless you can categorically confirm they are. Even if the SO had said this, he should have challenged them and confirmed the inmate's presence one way or the other.

I asked the SO what actually happened and he told me a much simpler version: 'He told me there were a couple of blocked spyholes. I told him he could either go back and do a proper roll check, or fuck off back to Albany. He chose the latter!'

So, in May 2013 when told I would now be working at Albany, it would be fair to say I wasn't keen in spite of the fact that Albany was considered by most Parkhurst officers to be a cushy posting, one that a number of my colleagues would have jumped at the chance of working in. But I didn't feel that way – I would have liked to have stayed at Parkhurst.

Albany was home to cat Bs, VPs (vulnerable prisoners) and sex offenders, and it was the sex offenders that I did not particularly want to work with. But the powers that be decided that after twenty-one years, this was the perfect time for me to go and work exclusively with rapists, gang rapists, necrophiliacs, beastophiles, gerontophiles, paedophiles and generally some of the most extreme sex offenders in the country.

There had been a strange meeting at Parkhurst where I'd been cross-examined on why I had not been at work the previous week on a day I was down as being on leave. I had pointed this out and even after we'd got hold of the detail office and were looking at a copy of that week's detail, confirming I was on leave, I was told that if in the future I was ever to be on leave then I needed to phone the prison to tell them I was not on duty. I'd been around long enough to know that sometimes your face just doesn't fit any more. This was right in the middle of the period in which the prison service 'paid off' a huge number of more senior prison officers, some 7000 in total. Soon after this episode, I was informed I had been transferred.

When I was initially informed of my move to Albany, I of course asked around, tried to find out about the place and apart from the fact that I was apparently a 'lucky twat to get such a cushy posting', it quickly became clear that Albany was a very particular kind of cat B men's prison. As one former officer told me, the full spectrum of inmates was there from paedophiles to gerontophiles and anything in between. For a start, he told me that I would have to get my head round the fact that thirty to forty of the blokes 'do their bird' as women, dressing and living as women. I had no problem with this in principle but I also believed in the first commandment of inmates – if there was a rule, they'd find a way to turn it to their advantage.

A few weeks before I knew that I was to be transferred to Albany there had been an escape attempt; apparently two inmates in adjoining cells had very nearly broken out from their cells by breaking through the outside walls. Fortunately, however, they had been grassed up and discovered. The holes that they dug were impressive and very nearly big enough for each of them to squeeze through. They were just behind the heating pipes and were made with a couple of small weights nicked from the gym, taking full advantage of the fact that there was a staff shortage owing to the recent exodus of experienced staff. While the government had decided that the prison service had a surplus of seemingly expensive officers, the inmates obviously benefited with such a shortfall of staff. Every wing in the country was now so short of staff, discipline was consequently just one of the things that could not be maintained, observation and monitoring were also in short supply. The inmates knew it and as usual were adept at taking full advantage of anything that was ripe and ready for exploitation.

Entering Albany for the first time was a strange experience. For a start, even though Parkhurst was so close, I could see it from pretty much everywhere. At Albany, I was, to all intents and purposes, starting from scratch. I was a new prison officer again. When I reached the gate, I was quite rightly asked for proof of my identity so I showed the gate staff my ID card and informed them that I was transferring from Parkhurst. When asked which wing I was going to be working on, I had to tell them that I didn't know. All I had been told was that I was now no longer working at Parkhurst and was to report to the Albany gate, but no more than that. But it turned out they knew even less than me and hadn't even been told I was arriving. Normally a prison officer would at least have a familiarisation visit, a walk-round guided tour, but so short of staff were the two prisons now that it seemed an Albany officer couldn't be spared.

Several phone calls were made and as it became clear that no one had actually been told where I was scheduled to work, it was decided to stick me on E wing. *Great, E wing. Where's that?* So, one of the gate staff escorted me there, where I found that as I was the 'early start' (the first officer on duty), I was responsible for relieving the night man. I was therefore on duty on a new wing in a new prison an hour before anyone else who actually knew anyone on the wing. My instincts were already screaming at me that this was a massive potential fuckup. Back in Parkhurst, the inmates would have smelt blood with a new face on the wing.

After the morning roll check (where the inmates on the wing were counted, signed for and the roll reported to the control room), I was given very brief instructions on how to get on to the landing, using a system called 'night san'. Now this was totally new to me: a system that allowed each of the four landings to be 'locked off'. This would allow one inmate to come out of his cell and use the toilet.

He had seven minutes to use the loo and then had to be back in his cell with the door locked, which could only be done from inside the cell once his door was shut. This system had been installed because the unfortunate design of each wing on Albany meant it was impossible to install the obligatory internal cell sanitation because of something to do with plumbing and pipework. Now I'm a technophobe at the best of times and 7.30 on a Sunday morning in a new prison on a new wing was really not the best time to show me how to do something like that. I thought I'd better just go and have a quick run-through, a quick practice just in case. As I approached the box containing the buttons that needed pushing and lights that needed flashing,

I caught sight of an inmate on the landing. After twenty-plus years this was a little unnerving: to have a prisoner out during 'patrol state' went against every instinct I had as a prison officer. An inmate out of his cell and walking along the landing was one thing, but an inmate wearing a ladies' dressing gown, Alice band and what looked like nail varnish waving at me was all too much. I decided my senses were overloaded and I needed a brew.

Now any self-respecting prison officer always carries an emergency brew kit made up of either a couple of teabags or coffee sachets. I had learned a very long time ago to drink black coffee as arriving on a wing and trying to scrounge a brew is fraught with problems because of the 'tea boat'. The tea boat is the tea-making area, usually stocked up with tea, coffee, milk and sugar, run by the staff who work on a particular wing. Some wings (very few, thankfully) don't even have one and this has always seemed to me to be a symptom of an unhappy group of staff, lacking a certain *esprit de corps* and group harmony. You should be able to trust each other with your lives, never mind paying for milk, tea, coffee and sugar.

Even if they have a tea boat, the politics can be a mine-field. Some wings, you can help yourself, sometimes you have to drop a few coins in to help run it. In my opinion the tea boat is one of the most important things on a wing, up there with the emergency exits, alarm bells and fire appliances as one of the first things to find on any new wing. You don't want your first impression of a new wing to be a hot drink faux pas. So, being not only on a new wing but in a new prison and with enough experience to know to bring my own stash, I made my way to find the kettle, reasoning that I needed a strong coffee immediately.

I was just making myself a brew when I heard the gate being unlocked and a regular E wing officer arrived. After introducing myself, I was immediately transported back some twenty-one years ago to 1992 when my self-introduction was met with an equally frosty reception. Some things in the prison service never change. I wondered if I had, without realising it, given exactly the same response to all the NEPOs I'd encountered at Parkhurst.

As the other officers started to arrive I was lucky that one or two had at least known I was coming and as officers are wont to do, they had made a phone call or several to check up on me. This involved phoning someone who knew someone who knew of me. They had decided from what they'd heard that I might be sort of all right (which I thought was good, if only because it meant I might be able to use their tea boat). This was common practice throughout the service. The first thing that happened when someone new arrived, whether a new governor or officer, was that phone calls were made to someone who knows someone who worked with them or knows of them to find out what they were like. The main reason for this, other than prison officers being professionally nosy, was that the prison service has a long and traditional penchant for the famous 'sideways move'. The ever-popular and ubiquitous sideways move usually happens when someone has fucked up and rather than any formal disciplinary action being taken, which might end up with a demotion, dismissal, etc., it was seen as better to remove the problem, keep it quiet and sweep it under the carpet or, to put it more succinctly, give the problem to someone else.

(Later the officer who had given me my initial frosty reception said, 'Sorry about earlier but I thought you were a NEPO!')

Albany, I quickly realised, was certainly very different. For a start we didn't have to actually unlock. The cell doors were unlocked remotely by the control room and as soon as the cell doors were unlocked, the wing office had a queue of inmates waiting outside. Now I had heard that sex offenders and their ilk were a tad needy but I had no idea how needy. As I watched a queue of inmates in a variety of outfits you'd never see at Parkhurst queuing up to make their case, I decided that Albany was going to be both a massive culture shock and a challenge.

I learned a long time ago to say nothing, watch and take it all in. Every wing I have ever worked in does it differently, each has its own subtly different rules and habits. Any wing might be next to and literally joined to another wing and yet have a totally different feel. For example, B wing and G wing at Parkhurst are connected – you can literally see the inmates and staff of each other's wing and the staff even share the same tea boat and cloakroom – but the way they do things is poles apart. Joining any new wing, the big mistake would be to say 'we don't do it like that' or 'it's better to do it this way'. So now that I was at Albany, I was trying to adopt that same policy but on that first day when the umpteenth inmate asked 'what time's exercise?', 'have the Avon catalogues been delivered?' or commented, 'oh, you must be new, you'll like it here', I started to think things were certainly done differently.

Doing the daily LBBs, or as they had recently been rebranded AFCs, was very different at Albany.[1] For a start, there was only one officer per landing and the cells were a lot smaller and without any form of sanitation other

---

1 Accommodation fabric check.

than a chemical khazi (a small portable toilet), meaning there were no double-occupancy cells. However, the ways that some inmates chose to live led to some of the cells being surprisingly feminine. Even if the perfume choice tended to make your eyes water and was more cheap market stall than Chanel No5, I had to admit it was a lot better than some of the festering hellholes I'd seen at Parkhurst![2]

Before I got to Albany, I had been forewarned that many of the inmates enjoy what was euphemistically called an 'alternative' lifestyle; many were openly homosexual and many identified as transgender. I'm a simple man who had never thought deeply about the complex interplay of gender, biological sex and identity, but from what I could glean, many of these inmates were women imprisoned inside a male body, which was then in turn imprisoned inside a men's prison. The many different types of inmate meant a veritable minefield of rules and regulations and certain protocol had to be followed.

I was used to searching a man's cell, I knew all the places things could be hidden in this set of kit, but this was a whole new world. Now I was rummaging around through ladies' smalls, make-up bags and high-heeled shoes, padded bras, wigs and 'sophisticated prostheses' including an item of underwear that I had never previously heard of: 'gaff pants'. These bespoke undergarments are apparently designed for the discerning drag queen or cross-dresser and are a pair of prosthetic panties that come with a silicon insert for that realistic camel-toe appearance and a rather

---

2   It was a low bar, admittedly, but you found yourself grateful not to find a pot full of assorted toenails, earwax and other things.

nifty testicle hiding area. And of course, anywhere that things could be hidden needed to be searched.

It was as if every situation I'd learned to deal with at Parkhurst needed a whole new way of thinking about it at Albany.

Code red

One morning early on at Albany, two of us arrived on the wing for the early shift. Usually only one officer did the early start but two makes doing the roll check easier. Frank, an officer I knew from working shifts at Parkhurst, went up to count the threes and fours while I did the ones and twos. We would then meet in the middle, confirm our total number of inmates to the control room, sign the ACCTs (Assessment, Care in Custody and Teamwork documents) and then sign again to say we'd signed everything and that the number of inmates was correct. The plan was once I'd finished the twos, I'd look up and see how Frank was getting on. That particular morning, he still had a few to do but he beckoned me up.

'Here, Mr B, have a butcher's – something doesn't look right.'

I went to the hatch and the first thing I noticed was that the bed was empty and unmade, the inmate apparently asleep on the floor. This in itself wasn't unusual. I'd known plenty of inmates who, for whatever reason, preferred to sleep on the floor. However, he had no bedding, not even a pillow, and was at a peculiar angle.

We knocked a few times, switched his light on and off and he hadn't even groaned. I tapped the door loudly with my keys and he didn't flinch, twitch or turn over.

We looked at each other then called it in, giving the cell number and name, the time and that the inmate was unresponsive on the floor of his cell and that Frank and I were both there and we were going to unlock and to check. Any time you go into a cell, it could be an ambush and you don't do it without following proper procedure. I trusted Frank and he knew the inmate, so I felt like we were OK. However, if it did go pear-shaped and it turned out he wanted a fight or needed emergency assistance, we needed permission. O1 radioed back that permission and informed the control room that we could proceed with caution and that he was on his way to assist.

Unlocking the cell door at night and entering is never as easy as it is later during the day. Nine times out of ten, inmates put something behind their doors at night – some sort of crude early warning system, I suppose. This time it was a chair with a plastic jug on it. We managed to push the door open while sliding the chair without the jug falling, but it was immediately obvious something was very wrong. The inmate, a young lad in his early to mid-twenties was ashen with a grey, clammy prison pallor, and seemingly out cold. He was cold to the touch, with blood on his fingertips and blood around his mouth, dressed only in prison-issue blue boxers, a strip of torn cloth around his chest.

Frank immediately checked the carotid pulse at the side of the inmate's neck. I called it in, stating it was a 'code red'. After finding no pulse, we checked and again found nothing. We both checked for a radial pulse at the wrist, felt nothing and the inmate's breathing was shallow, very shallow. We looked at each other and started immediate CPR. On the TV, this always looks quite relaxed but in real life for it to do any good, you really have to give it some welly. One first aid instructor told me he'd never successfully given chest compressions without breaking at least a couple of ribs! Luckily, it was only a few minutes before the medics arrived and got stuck in and the youngster was taken out to hospital.

The paramedics patted Frank on the shoulder as they left.

'Well done, lads, you starting on the CPR almost certainly saved his life.'

Not for the first time I thought what a strange thing it was to that person. You didn't think about the crime, about what they might have done, you just went in and did what you had to do. I had never seen an attack or suicide attempt that resulted in blood around the mouth and fingers and was genuinely mystified.

By this point, the other staff were arriving and while they finished off the roll check, Frank and I went through the prison officer's finely-honed procedure of brews and paperwork. It was just as we were finishing the reams of paperwork that the governor came in with an update: the inmate was alive, just! The blood around his mouth was not blood, as we had assumed, but lipstick and the bloodied fingertips were, in fact, nail varnish.

I realised that I had to unlearn all my assumptions from Parkhurst.

Meetings

Governors love meetings, or at least that's how it seems to prison officers. If they don't love them, they must be utterly miserable as they seem to spend their whole lives in them. Over the last few decades the job of governor has been transformed and now involves hardly any time on the wing. Being a humble prison officer can sometimes feel like being a prehistoric villager waiting for the holy men to tell you what the Gods have decreed. At Albany, I quickly learned that this was even more the case than Parkhurst.

One particular day we were gathered together to hear the decision made at a recent meeting. After much careful consideration and deliberation, it had been decided that concrete planters could be placed on HB 17's exercise yard.[3] Apparently, it was hoped that these would be an aesthetically pleasing focal point. At Parkhurst, prior to the exercise period, the entire exercise area was searched thoroughly, checking the integrity of the perimeter and any items that might have been dropped and forgotten, and that the enterprising inmate might find useful. Once this was done, the control room was informed and the necessary box ticked. If this meant a little bit less time while the exercise area was properly checked, so be it. If someone at Parkhurst had had the bright idea of creating an entirely new set of hiding places, complete with soil to dig and hide things in, it's highly likely it would have been shot down by one of the senior officers – at least there would have been a chance for the officers to give their opinion.

Albany, as I quickly found out, did things a little differently. Once the decision had been made, the concrete planters – which were to be actually made in the prison – needed to be put in place immediately. But first, there needed to be another meeting to decide where exactly on the yard they should be placed and more importantly, how

---

3   HB stands for House Block – a new name for wing – which it had been decided was far too austere and draconian and was upsetting the inmates. Sorry, 'residents'.

many there should be. Once that was decided, there needed to be a conversation about how big they were going to be. They went for three foot long, a foot wide, with a foot depth. The day came and the planters arrived, already nicely full of an assortment of low-maintenance colourful plants. Even I had to admit that they looked rather lovely. I reckon they stayed that way for about a week after which the constant digging and prodding and poking as officers carefully searched the entirety of the soil for hidden objects ruined the plants and we were left with a selection of ugly, squat concrete boxes. A couple of months after the plants went in, there was another meeting and another governor came walking through the yard.

'What on earth are those?' they asked.

The officer started to explain that they were an aesthetically pleasing focal point but was told in no uncertain terms that the concrete boxes needed to be removed immediately as they were a very real danger, could be used as some sort of battering ram against the gate and/or smashed and broken up and the rubble used as projectiles. They were, he said, a serious risk to the health and safety of both staff and inmates. So, in they came and took them away again. Here, in a way I'd not encountered before, there was a huge tension between the idea of prison as a place that, in essence, shouldn't be very nice and the idea that for prisoners to be rehabilitated, you had to make it as nice as possible.

One time, an inmate had an improvised weapon, described as looking like a hunting knife. He had threatened staff with it, a consequence of which meant that the inmate had to be restrained. The weapon was removed, as was the inmate, who during the adjudication pleaded not guilty, citing in mitigation that he only had it for protection because there were bullies on the wing. The powers that be had missed the point entirely – that the so-called piece of protective equipment was in fact used as an offensive weapon and that it had, in fact, been used to threaten officers. Instead, the governor concentrated on the fact that there were bullies on the wing.

In reality, there are bullies and bullying on each and every wing but the culture of silence means there's very little you can actually do about it unless someone is willing to formally complain, rather than saying 'I walked into a door, Guv'; all we can try and do is minimise the opportunity for it. The one thing I know that does that is a staffing level that allows for regular and thorough checks all over a prison. It's not rocket science. If you don't have that, there are places you can't monitor and it's in these places that inmates will see an opportunity. Officers can't place an inmate on report because of a suspicion. Evidence is needed. However, none of this was addressed in this instance. Instead, in an attempt to put the tooled-up, threatening inmate's safety first, the nicking was thrown out. Again and again, to me it seemed as if the cart was being put before the horse, the tail wagging the dog, and generally people without enough experience of inmates on the wing were driving prison policy.

One morning, staff attended one of the daily morning briefings, where the governor filled the staff in on the previous night's shenanigans. Someone had apparently crapped on the landing and had used the resulting by-product to write obscenities, threats and racial slurs on a couple of the cell doors.

The morning meeting was also used as an opportunity to remind staff that they were obliged to respect an inmate's gender identity, as a lot of staff in this cat B male prison were referring to inmates as being 'male'. The governor went on to say that this had to stop, and stop immediately. From then on, if Nigel wanted to be called Nigella, Benjamin, Brenda, and Philip, Philippa, that was how they were to be addressed. Failure to adhere to this would result in disciplinary action being taken. Any questions? It was a tumbleweed moment until one wily old screw put his hand up and asked if the ability to change names applied to staff as well. They clearly hadn't been prepared for that particular question and fumbled over an answer, the gist of which was that, when all officers had epaulette numbers to identify them, it didn't seem necessary and why was he asking?

'Well, what if I've been thinking I'd like to be known as Victoria Sponge?'

'And why would that be?' asked the governor, completely confused now.

'It was as a small personal homage to my favourite cake,' came the immediate reply.

As you can imagine, the place erupted into laughter as the governor attempted to keep order in the midst of a major sense of humour failure. It became clear that there was a real generation divide within prison staff and this was a neat example of it. The room was split between those who really didn't think inmates should be writing in shit on the walls – and those who were really interested in what the writing said.

There was an alarm bell on D wing (sorry, House Block 12) and as half a dozen of us were approaching the wing, we could already hear shouting, with threats and multiple 'fucks' being thrown around. It was one of those situations that you instinctively knew was only ever going to end badly. There was a stand-off with some of the inmates and it was the exact moment that we entered the wing that seemed to be the trigger point, because as soon as half a dozen screws appeared on the scene, the whole tense situation ignited.

One inmate made a threatening move to an officer and was immediately taken down by two officers, then a second inmate lashed out and had to be restrained. At this, the spectators became a baying crowd, angry, threatening, abusive and violent. Three or four made a move to help the two inmates and were held back. The first inmate was punching, head-butting, spitting and snarling, seemingly high on something, and was proving difficult to restrain – not helped by his muscle-packed bulk. He was short, squat and powerful, with his body pumped full of who knows what, and spoiling for a fight. The two officers were in a desperately shitty situation.

I immediately went to assist them, the other officers either went to assist in the restraining of the two inmates or crowd control. But I was struggling with the super-strong inmate, as were the other two officers. He was incredibly angry, spitting, snarling and seemingly immune to pain; he was also sweating profusely, making it difficult – if not impossible – to get a grip. Somehow in the struggle I ended up beneath the inmate, who was now trying to bite and head-butt me. The other two officers managed to move him just long enough for me to wriggle free, but not before the inmate had sunk his teeth into my side. At this point a couple of other officers arrived and managed to sort of get control.

I was just checking the impressive array of teeth marks on my love handles, while thinking how the hell was I going to explain them to my wife, when I heard a commotion towards the wing entrance. It seemed the situation was escalating, and escalating fast. I walked to the source of this new melee just in time to see an officer being escorted away from it with a nasty-looking head injury. Meanwhile two hugely experienced officers were wrestling another monster-size inmate, trying to hold him and keep him down and away from the officer he had just assaulted. Once again, I had little or no choice but to help restrain this other inmate. We eventually managed to somehow control him. Luckily, like most muscle-bound monsters do, he tired incredibly quickly and we basically managed to rope-a-dope him until more staff arrived and therefore managed to de-escalate what could have been an extremely serious situation.

I was being checked over by the medics when I heard a couple of the other officers talking about the total lack of backup by some of the NEPOs. Here were these young, fit recruits standing by and letting the old blokes do all the work. One especially had been filming on his body worn camera and three (that I saw) were watching. Later, questions were asked about their lack of involvement. One of them actually had the temerity to say that they had been told not to get involved unless absolutely neces-sary (and they apparently didn't deem it necessary) as they thought we had it under control. Another even said that the governors previously stated, 'If it kicks off, leave it to the experienced officers.' The trouble with this thinking was that the 'experienced' officers were usually by that very definition more than double the age of the youngsters (in the case of the second inmate that I helped restrain, the three of us officers had a combined age of 172, the youngest being fifty-one) and the younger staff were often not getting the experience which would in turn build confidence. At some point, those fifty-one-year-olds just wouldn't be there any more and then you would have a generation of 'experienced' officers, none of whom knew what to do when it kicked off.

A couple of days later, I was standing by the treatment hatches at lunch, trying to keep an eye on the toing and froing, when crash, bang, wallop, the two inmates in front of me started trading punches. I stepped between them but the punches continued; I was trying to separate them and watch for any weapon, telling them in no uncertain terms to calm down and stop what they were doing immediately (well, that's the family-friendly version!). They were getting more aggressive, with one trying to bite the other, so I had one against the wall and a handful of sweatshirt of the other but couldn't raise the alarm or use my radio.

It was then that I saw Stan holding on to the gate, watching.

'Hit the bell,' I said, noticing that my colleague had neither his phone nor a radio close to hand.

In fact, they were both on the small table behind them and well within reach of the inmates he was supposed to be watching.

He didn't react.

'HIT THE FUCKING BELL!' I shouted.

This finally had the desired effect. Within seconds, backup arrived and the fighting inmates were removed. O1 asked what had happened and I explained about the two combatants but didn't mention Stan and his reluctance to raise the alarm. Once the situation was resolved and we finally finished, I pulled him to one side.

'What the fuck was that about, Stan? Why didn't you raise the alarm?'

He just looked sheepish.

'It seemed like you had things under control.'

'And why the fuck didn't you have your radio on you? Why was it on the desk?'

'It's a bit uncomfortable, like,' he said, gesturing to his waist. 'It digs into my side.'

Fire, fire!

A few years into my time at Albany, one of the prisoners decided to set fire to a landing on the threes. Though the staff reacted quickly, they were prevented from getting on to the actual landing because for whatever reason, whether a technical glitch, faulty or fucked either way, the locking mechanism was fucked so the staff were stuck behind a locked door. Thick and acrid, the smoke was getting thicker and causing even more problems in an already problematic situation. The situation was rapidly getting out of hand.

Eventually we got on to the landing but not before the intensity of the heat from the fire, which the fire starter had been enthusiastically feeding, fuelled with bedding, clothing, bins and even TVs, had ignited the landing above. Once we had got on to the landing, we crawled through the smoke and flames, removed the arsonist and evacuated and accounted for each and every inmate; a number of the prisoners and a few of us officers were taken to hospital suffering from smoke inhalation. It had been a close thing, but we were lucky indeed not to have lost a single life.

The prisoner responsible got an extra five years for very nearly killing a wing full of prisoners and staff. Fast-forward seven years . . . Some of those prisoners who were rescued by the staff won a compensation claim. The staff, who had run on to a smoke-filled flaming inferno of a landing, released and rescued up to forty-eight prisoners, got them off the wing and to a place of safety, did not receive a penny.

If you were to design an experiment where you filled a building full of the most cunning people in society and then gave them the tools to engineer claims for compensation, it would be hard to do it better than this. Compensating a prisoner with taxpayers' money for a fellow inmate's actions is something that is readily and so obviously ripe for exploitation to anyone who's worked on a wing, it hurts. Through an accident of timing, I spent the last ten years of my career at a prison with a very different culture but I know that these issues were coming up everywhere, including Parkhurst.

CHAPTER 9

A Brave New World

It was the floppy, knitted colander on Phil's head that did it. The governor spotted it immediately and came sailing over.

'Remove that thing please, officer.'

'I'm afraid I can't, Guv,' said Phil, his face full of regret. 'It's part of my religion.'

'Don't be ridiculous, man. Take it off this minute.'

The governor's face was already turning a deep shade of angry puce.

'I'm a newly ordained minister in the Church of the Flying Spaghetti Monster,' he added, the governor's face getting pinker with every word. 'A Pastafarian,' he added, helpfully. He even offered to get his Certificate of Ordination from the office.

'It's not standard uniform, take it off. Immediately.'

'Inmates of many religions are allowed to wear their respective headwear, Guv. Jewish inmates wear the kippah, Muslims, their taqiyah, Sikhs, their turbans, Rastafarians, the rastacap. The knitted colander is a sacred marker of my faith and I won't be discriminated against.'

The governor just stood looking at him, shaking with anger.

'Besides,' Phil added helpfully, 'I made sure it was in black, to go with the uniform.'

'You can either take it off this minute or you can go home.'

Phil cheerfully went home and the governor went off to take his blood pressure medication.

★

Phil was a wind-up merchant but there was something serious at the heart of what he'd done. During my last years in prison, an entire culture of absolute care and respect towards inmates had come to define the prison experience. And as with anything in prison, this culture was massively open to abuse as inmates took advantage of anything they could.

The new culture came in, inch by inch, tradition by tradition. Cells became 'rooms', inmates became 'residents' with their own choice of preferred gender pronouns, prison officers became 'care workers or case officers', wings were 'House Units' or 'House Blocks', in-cell . . . sorry, 'in-room'. Telephones and televisions in cells also became common. Officers now had to knock on an inmate's cell door, seeking permission to enter. A list of carefully considered saccharine-sweet policies all engineered to help soften the blow of the once-austere, horrendously unpleasant life behind bars. It seemed to me as if the trail of victims, of damage and destruction, didn't matter. The idea that the criminal is made a little uncomfortable during their time inside seemed suddenly alien. It didn't matter if they were a murderer, rapist, paedophile, terrorist, kidnapper or fraudster, it became the prison's job to be as pleasant an experience as possible, accommodating and caring, and the prison staff's role was to deliver this softer service.

My time working in prisons splits neatly into just over twenty years at Parkhurst and almost a decade at Albany as a finale. Who knows what I'd think if I'd stayed at Parkhurst my entire career, whether the changes might have seemed less stark? But one thing that was true was that every single one of the senior staff I had worked with during my time at Parkhurst had had some sort of working life prior to becoming a prison officer. For some it was just a few years in a different career, for others a whole career, but they brought some sense of life and its realities. Because it seems like an obvious thing to say but prison inmates aren't like the general public. They are by definition the people who through their actions have taken themselves out of circulation, who have done things we agree as a society should be met with prison time. Now you can argue all you want about the fairness of the process that got them there and plenty of much cleverer people than me do, but once they're inside, the job requires people with a certain ability to suspect the worst of a situation. Because if you place a bet that every inmate you meet is a misunderstood sweetheart, you're very quickly going to lose – and lose big.

In my experience, a healthy amount of cynicism seems to rise with an exposure to life outside of an academic environment. Nowadays, the prison service seems reluctant to employ experienced people, instead preferring to employ the untarnished youngster, those unsullied by life's harsh realities. It is without doubt now the case that a tech-savvy twenty-year-old versed in all sorts of sociological theory is seen as a much greater potential asset to the service than someone who has served their time at the school of life.

Along with a lack of real-world experience, the new generation of officers are often extremely confident in their own ability, more relaxed and very ready to not do something they don't want to. When I started working as a prison officer, I had to grasp things and grasp them quickly: if I fucked up, I would be told in no uncertain terms that I had done so and if I fucked up again, I would be told I was a useless cunt who's fucked up again. If you kept on fucking things up, you got the message that you weren't in the right place or the right job. It was understood this was the fucker-up's fault, they were definitely not right for the role. Now, even a whiff of that old-school culture and you'd be under investigation for bullying. Years ago, if you were given a job to do, you did it; if you did it badly, you stayed on that job until you got the hang of it. Countless times I've seen a NEPO given a job to do, only to say they don't want to do it and if you try and make them, the officer is a bully. I once saw an officer reprimanded because they informed a colleague that they were going to have to go on exercise duty for the full hour and a half. They were told that a junior colleague was not going to do this as it was freezing cold, windy and raining heavily and they had been to the hairdresser's the day before. In many ways, this is a change that has happened across society, so why wouldn't it happen in prisons too? But in prison, the stakes are so much higher.

The determination to do, or at least appear to do the right thing – the politically correct thing – is on the one hand theoretically and morally commendable. Every prison officer knows that you can only make a wing work with give and take, a mixture of discipline and humanity. If you go into the prison service and decide that you're going to treat inmates like animals, you won't last a week. However, the constant move in this direction is very often detrimental, especially when you have people at the top of the service so terrified of being drawn into possible scandal that they make baffling decisions.

Pull the other one

A couple of years ago, I heard a story about an inmate at another prison. It turned out they had a bit of a penchant for interior decorating, specifically soft furnishings. They'd asked their family to send in some muslin curtains. This is not as unusual as it sounds – inmates these days are allowed curtains as it's thought to be something to personalise their cell, brighten things up a bit and add an element of comfort. To the prison officer, it's just one more thing that needs to be constantly searched, one more source of material for suicide attempts, one more thing to get tangled in if things kick off, or to be burnt in a cell fire. It's also one more thing to argue, negotiate and bargain over with all the attendant paperwork and potential for criticism of that paperwork.

On this particular occasion, the muslin curtains turned up at reception. However, they were far too long and not fire retardant. Basically, they didn't meet a few of the criteria so the inmate wasn't allowed to have them in his cell. They would, he was informed, be kept in his stored property and returned to him on release or transfer. He was, it would be fair to say, not a happy bunny. These were expensive, and a very specific sort of soft muslin curtains. As far as he was concerned, he was allowed these curtains and it was unacceptable for the screws to deny him them. Fortunately, he was not the type of inmate who had a short fuse or one who used aggression to get his own way. The subtle silent approach was more his modus operandi and so the form filling began.

The staff gritted their teeth for a long boring process in which the extremely clear and sensible prison rules were upheld but the result on this occasion was pretty quick and not what they had expected. The governor overruled the decision by the reception staff and informed the inmate in no uncertain terms that he could indeed have the curtains in his cell. What's more, the reception staff were wholly out of order to deny him those curtains.

The reception senior officer was unhappy with the governor's decision, which was in complete contrast to the prison service rules regarding curtains, and challenged him about it. The governor stated that the decision was final because the reception staff could not deny the inmate his curtains simply because he was a Muslim. This would be the punchline to a joke if it didn't reveal the thinking behind hundreds of bad decisions being made every day.

Prison isn't everyday society. You can't just impose things that work in society wholesale in a prison. Foul language, threatening behaviour and extreme piss-taking occur in a way that they don't outside of prison. If you start judging prison by those standards, it will always come up short.

I've seen people horrified by an experienced prison officer addressing an inmate's request with 'fuck off and fuck off now'. You can see the wheels in their heads turning: of course men behave brutally if we treat them like brutes. It feels like something that can be fixed immediately. If we fix the way we speak to residents, then we'll see an improvement in behaviour. However, generations of prison officers have grown up talking to generations of inmates. That kind of definitive, unambiguous tone, complete with judicious swear words, works. It's how inmates speak to each other, it's very often language they grew up with and understood and spoke, how the men they respected talked to each other. Nothing's going to get an inmate's antennae for a potential weakness in the team than someone coming in and saying,

'Excuse me, my good man, but would you mind vacating this particular area post-haste?' OK, you wouldn't speak to someone like this outside, in the boardroom, or the university lecture theatre. But this isn't outside, it's prison. You can't impose the rules of one on the other. You can object to zoos in principle all you want, but once you find yourself in the lions' cage, you'd better fucking listen to the zookeeper!

New generation

Don't get me wrong, some of the new recruits were brilliant, keen, willing and able, however they were very definitely in the minority. Around eight out of ten new recruits I met just seemed fundamentally unsuited to the job. One day an inmate had to be put behind his door because he had made one of the new female officers cry. This crying thing was new to me. I had been in the job, working on a landing or wing, for over twenty years before I ever saw or heard of an officer crying, but now it had become a regular occurrence. New inexperienced staff would often burst into tears or storm off, unable to deal with the harsh realities of prison life. Whether it was because an inmate's budgie had died, someone had crapped on the floor, or they couldn't deal with blood, or just because an inmate had been a bit mean, there was a long list of reasons for them to cry.

This particular inmate was a nasty piece of work, a misogynist bully, and what he'd said to the female officer had been out of order. Of course, the rules around respect only flowed in one direction and there was no way that we'd be able to report him for something he'd apparently said to an officer, though if the officer concerned had said the equivalent thing to him they'd have been in trouble.

By happy accident, a couple of days after the incident I had the rather unpleasant task of escorting the inmate to hospital. He had a nasty-looking cyst on the back of his neck that needed to be looked at. I was cuffed to him and fortunately for me, he was quiet, unusually so for this gobshite. The reason for his subdued demeanour became apparent when the doctor called us into the examination room. The inmate was shitting himself – he didn't like needles and thought he was going to die. Worried the cyst was cancerous, he asked the doctor repeatedly if he was going to die. The doctor made all the right noises and said all the complicated medical things that doctors say, but said they'd need further tests to be sure.

While walking out of the hospital to the agreed pick-up spot, I saw one of my former colleagues from Parkhurst with an inmate who was in a wheelchair. An overweight, diabetic junkie, he had been at the hospital for a couple of weeks after having one of his legs amputated owing to his diabetes. He sat in the wheelchair with his freshly acquired stump on full display. I said hello to the officer, asked how he was doing and we caught up for a minute or so while waiting for our transport back to the prison.

When they were gone, the inmate I was cuffed to turned to me: 'Is he from Parkhurst then, Guv?'

He was still shaky from the doctor's office.

'Yep,' I said.

'What happened to his leg?' he asked.

'Well, it's an interesting story, actually,' I said. 'He's been in and out of hospital for months now, having an awful time, in agony most of the time. They've cut one leg off, they may well have to take the other one off too.'

'Fuck!' he said, shaking his head.

'And to think it all started off as a small cyst on the back of his neck.'

He sat in silence the whole way back and went back to his cell as good as gold. The principal officer was shocked that an inmate who was normally disruptive at every opportunity was so quiet.

'What the fuck happened to him?'

'I don't think he likes doctors,' I told him.

I may be proved absolutely wrong – in many ways, I really hope I am. We might see an age of mutual respect ushered in by the new generation, which transforms prison into a therapeutic space where true rehabilitation can occur. The role of prison officer might become a dream job, requiring multiple degrees. Children might turn to their mothers and say, 'Mummy, when I grow up, I want to be a prison officer.' But we're certainly not there yet.

I was due to retire from the prison service at the age of sixty, however I left the service some six months early. I could have chosen to work until I was sixty-seven, but by the time I left, I hated the job and what it had become. I knew it was time to go when an inmate asked me a simple question, 'Guv, when's our library?' and I didn't know the answer. Dancing to a tune played by government, governors were changing things so regularly it was almost weekly. Inmates and officers like structure and routine yet we were always kept off balance. It felt as far away from the prison service I'd joined all those years before as possible. Within two months of starting my job at Parkhurst, I knew the library times, the exercise times, visits and gym times and the times of each session. There was a culture that there was huge value in the way things had been done. As a junior officer, you absorbed the accumulated wisdom of all the prison officers who had come before you. The reasoning was that if a procedure had stood up to the tens of thousands of the country's finest criminal minds and they hadn't found a way to fuck with it, it was probably a good procedure worth keeping. Did this mean that prison officers were sometimes resistant to change and kept on doing things just because that's the way they'd always been done? Possibly. But in my opinion we've thrown out multiple babies with the bathwater.

It's also true that large aspects of society have moved under our feet while I've been a prison officer. When I joined, the odd inmate who wanted to wear women's underwear wasn't unheard of.

In my later years as an officer, I was placed under investigation for allegedly 'torturing' an inmate. This particular inmate was a convicted sex offender who had decided that he now no longer wished to live as a man, so started to wear make-up and dresses, despite the fact that his name, according to the information on the computerised 'foolproof' records system, was Nicolas. His gender was recorded as male, he was fifty-three years old and in a cat B adult male prison and had not registered on the transgender pathway programme. Because of this, I had, on three separate occasions, referred to him with masculine pronouns: i.e. 'he', 'him' and 'his'. He made a formal complaint, stating that I had breached his fundamental human rights and had essentially subjected him to humiliation, bullying and torture. Additionally, and to save any confusion, I was reminded to refer to the inmates as 'residents'.

A couple of weeks after I had been read the riot act for my overly callous and cruel behaviour by a governor, we had a problem with one of the landings, who were refusing to 'bang up'. The officer who was fairly new to the job couldn't get the pissed-off inmates to go behind their doors. I went on to the landing, spoke to the inmates – and more importantly, listened – then I ooohed and aahed, ummed in the right places, shook my head and looked very concerned and full of empathy and sympathy to their desperate plight.[1] Eventually, and only after a lot of toing and froing, they decided that they had got their point across and consequently sauntered off and 'banged up'.

Now I didn't make a big deal of it as I only saw it as a potential problem as opposed to an actual problem, consequently I didn't overreact. As far as I was concerned it was job done. The wing roll wasn't late and we all went home. However, the very next day, one of the new generation of governors went and got themselves all busy on the wing. They approached me and said they'd heard that there was a bit of trouble on the wing the previous day. I genuinely hadn't considered what happened as noteworthy, so I replied 'Trouble? No, I don't think so – I was on the wing and nothing springs to mind.'

'That's not what I heard. I heard there were inmates who wouldn't bang up.'

'Oh yeah. They had a bit of a moan but went away after a bit,' I conceded.

---

1 The essence of which was that owing to staff shortages, they were receiving a lot less time out of their cells and were banged up for longer each day.

'I want you to nick the inmates who refused to go away and place them on report for concerted indiscipline.'

I let the governor know in no uncertain terms that I wasn't going to do that. For one, they had gone away. Two, no one but the officer in any given situation can decide to place an inmate on report. Basically, no one can tell you to 'nick' someone. It was a judgement call that I had made in the moment and I was sticking by it. If we started nicking inmates, ahem, 'residents' for this sort of thing, it would have been thirteen separate nickings this time. Then what would happen next time? What happened if it was ever serious? I'd far rather get them behind their doors by talking than threats of nickings. You'd just make a rod for your own back, lose credibility and end up never getting them away.

Within a week, I'd seen that they paid lip service to the humanity of inmates at a cosmetic level but not the underlying principle. Referring to someone by the wrong pronoun was a crime but the old prison skills of give and take, of treating an inmate with a bit of common-sense respect, allowing them to feel listened to for a moment, rather than needlessly throwing the rule book at them, that was of zero value in the modern prison regime.

A few days later, I received a strongly worded email from the governor, informing me that they were extremely disappointed I'd refused to put the men on report. I was very tempted to reply, 'Sir, I think you'll find that you've actually used the wrong pronoun as I think you'll find some of them identify as she/her.'

The general creep of softened rules was visible everywhere you looked.

The Seg staff were once in the process of locating an inmate in the Seg unit. This particular inmate was a fiery fucker, always argumentative, with an air of misguided self-importance; he hated authority and hated screws. When staff proceeded to do the obligatory strip search, he began to perform, shouting and arguing. This came to a head when an officer went through his eighteen-inch dreadlocks and found a small packet of cannabis. The inmate went mental, stating we had no right to search his dreads. In the old days this would have been laughed off but I know for a fact the officer was genuinely worried that they were going to be reprimanded – and had they been, none of us would have been surprised.

Shower time

One day, the cleaning officer had fed the wing and called for the stragglers not once but three times: the usual 'any more dinner', 'last call dinner', 'HOTPLATE CLOSING!'. Four inmates hadn't collected their meals, the hotplate (serving area) had been closed and it was then that the four turned up, just in time to be far too late. When told that it was now too late, they went fucking ballistic. They had just returned from the gym and decided that they needed a shower before collecting and eating their meal. However, they were told in no uncertain terms that they should have had the shower before they left the gym. Their argument was that they didn't have time and that the officer had said they could have a shower.

The officer in question was new, just turned twenty and ripe for exploitation. In the nine weeks that he had been an officer he had already got himself a reputation for his complete inability to use the word 'No'. When asked to confirm the fact that he gave permission, he said that he had indeed, because they had just got back from the gym and were covered in sweat. It was then pointed out to him that each and every gym session has a fifteen-minute built-in shower time. At this the officer said he knew that, but they hadn't had time. The inmates refused to bang up until they had had a meal, a meal to which they were entitled because they had a right to be fed.

Things escalated – and fast. Two inmates went behind their door without a meal and two others went down the block. The officer had caused a problem, a problem that should not have occurred and one that could have been avoided simply by using the word 'No'. This is what people without experience on wings don't understand. It might look like a small thing but the entire system relies on a very clear sense of firm boundaries. You should get the same answer from every officer because it's the rules. It shouldn't be up to individual officers to apply their own interpretation because that's a crack. One tiny crack in that façade and the inmates get into it, and they work away at that tiny crack until it's a breach.

Lions led by donkeys

Many years ago, when I started working at Parkhurst there would inevitably be trouble. This could be anything from a minor infraction of the prison rules to fights, fires or concerted indiscipline and on the odd occasion, all of the above at the same time. During these times, like anyone else, staff can get anxious, apprehensive, or dare I say, even a little scared. However, these volatile times were often when they were at their best. Professionals who worked well together, led by people who were well respected. There was a fundamental mutual respect between the leaders and the followers because the leaders had often been there and done it.

Experience and respect are in my opinion the two most important things any member of prison staff can have. Many a time someone with a higher rank would be in the thick of it with you, leading by example, and you were happy to follow as they led you into a shitstorm. Nowadays, however, someone from a higher rank is more likely to send you into a shitstorm and then complain about how you dealt with it. I vividly remember one particular instance when this happened. It was in the Seg unit with an inmate who had over a long period of time shown a propensity for violence, assaulting staff and other inmates for no other reason than he wanted to – he liked it, so he did it, hence him being in the Seg unit. On this occasion he had assaulted an officer, punching him so hard that the man was knocked out; he then started to kick him until other staff who heard the commotion turned up and raised the alarm. The inmate continued with his kicking spree and the three staff attempted to restrain him and prevent further injuries being inflicted.

The duty governor arrived and immediately told the staff to stop restraining the inmate as 'they were hurting him'. The now-comatose officer was bleeding, struggling to breathe and gurgling – his eyes had rolled to the back of his head so far that only the whites of his eyes were visible. A nurse arrived and was immediately directed to the officer. Again, the duty governor intervened, saying the inmate needed looking at.[2] The governor was so fixated

---

2 Shockingly, this is technically correct. The nurses are not obliged to tend to prison staff as the NHS contract with the prison service is for the sole care of inmates.

on the care and well-being of the inmate and so scared of the inmate making a formal complaint that the violent inmate became his only concern.

Very often we would arrive for work and pinned to the gate lodge window would be a note informing staff that a former colleague had sadly passed away. This happened far too many times. One day I turned up for work and yet another note was pinned to the gate lodge window, informing staff that 'It is with great sadness that we are able to inform you that Mr Donaldson has passed away after a short illness. Our thoughts and prayers are with his family, etc., etc.'. I had been at Parkhurst for over twenty years, so felt a bit guilty that for some reason I could not remember him. After racking my brains for a bit, I became totally flummoxed, so only after swallowing my pride, I asked a colleague, where did Mr Donaldson work and when did he retire? It was then that I was informed that he was in fact a con who had been on E wing.

Governors

Over the years I've had chance to work with some fantastic governors – governors whom I would have followed anywhere, governors who were fearless, often possessing a moral and professional integrity that was admired throughout the prison by staff and inmates. However, I've also had the misfortune to work with those governors who seemed only concerned with their own power.

One such governor, who shall remain anonymous (let's call him 'Governor X'), was a strange individual, universally disliked by just about everyone. Even the civilian staff were aware of his many shortcomings. Someone once described him by saying, 'You have to remember he is a small man with a big rank,' and that just about summed him up. Most people on initially meeting him would say that he came across as a likeable person, however this superficial likeability was always short-lived.

This particular governor suffered from a rather unfortunate condition, 'pseudologia fantastica': he was a pathological liar, he genuinely couldn't help himself. He lied to ingratiate himself with his peers, he lied to impress and he lied to get himself out of the shit, even though nine times out of ten, it was lies that got him there in the first place. The archetypal compulsive liar in other words. Though admittedly sometimes this was hugely entertaining, it was also dangerous, if only because of his position. Most of us are guilty of telling porkies, and normally those porkies are little more than harmless white lies, but the trouble with his compulsion was that he would happily drop someone in the shit to make himself look good, get himself out of trouble or sometimes where you couldn't see any advantage and just had to assume he enjoyed it. To paraphrase Winston Churchill on Stanley Baldwin, he would 'occasionally stumble over the truth, but hastily pick himself up and hurry on as if nothing had happened'.

Another governor I worked with was a bit of a contradiction – on the surface seemingly efficient, great at admin, and knew the rules and regulations inside and out. They could quote verbatim chapter and verse on any given prison service policy. Unfortunately, they were also confusingly contradictive, both parsimonious and generous. Parsimonious with praise, gratitude and thank yous, while overly generous with criticism and contempt. They seemed to possess a penchant for investigations after the event. Any event they'd been safely a long way from when it happened and they'd actually sent you into the shit. They were one of those 'man managers' who couldn't manage men, relishing the role and rank of governor, though seemingly despising the staff they actually governed.

He wasn't alone in his apparent disdain for prison officers, something I saw first-hand when a long-serving, highly respected officer was diagnosed with what turned out to be a life-limiting condition, which resulted in him having to be medically discharged from the service, a service he loved. Fortunately for the devastated officer and his family, the Guv was very sympathetic and made all the right noises. However, when the time came for the officer to finally and somewhat reluctantly leave the service, the governor, rather than pay him his full compensation payout – which after thirty years as a prison officer he was entitled to – decided for whatever reason, he would only pay him 75 per cent of the actual figure.

A long, lengthy and somewhat expensive appeal process took place and all while the officer was, by now, in extremely poor health, doubtless made worse by the fact that he was having to fight for what he was entitled to. They found in favour of the officer. The parsimonious governor finally and reluctantly paid 90 per cent of the full compensation package. This was an officer who had given their life to the service, who had been commended for bravery by the self-same governor, who then tried to stop them getting what was due to them. Someone had clearly plugged all of the experienced officers into a spreadsheet and decided they weren't offering value. The problem was, as often happens, the spreadsheet didn't have a column for any of the important things – it didn't show all the situations nipped in the bud by a quiet word in the right ear, or the rapes and assaults and killings avoided by an officer following instincts honed after twenty-plus years of experience. Instead, hundreds if not thousands of years of experience were lost from the service because they were too 'expensive'. Oscar Wilde once said, 'A fool is someone who knows the price of everything and the value of nothing.' Maybe he came up with that while in prison.

So poor were the staffing levels and the general level of experience on the wing that the powers that be came up with the brilliant idea of asking the inmates to hand anything in that they shouldn't have. A note was handed to each inmate asking that they hand in mobile phones, drugs, weapons, SIM cards, memory sticks, tobacco and porn. They were told that there would be no recriminations, questions or punishments related to anything put in the bin bag on that day, a twenty-four-hour amnesty.

I thought this was a terrible idea that signalled weakness and that we didn't have a clue what was going on. The inmates only had to have eyes in their heads to realise that we were short-staffed but this was advertising the fact. When the twenty-four hours was up and they checked the contents of the bin, they had received seven pairs of underpants (two of which had unidentified brown stains, two with unidentified white stains), four pairs of socks (two of which were odd), a toilet roll, a couple of empty plastic bottles that smelt as if they had at one time or another contained hooch, and three magazines (one of which was porn). The poor staff who had to go around with the bin bag were laughed out of every cell but the higher-ups decided it was the officers' fault for not being 'robust' enough that no actual illicit items were handed in.

Problem staff

One morning, one of the wing 'faces' came into the office, ranting and raving about getting a knock-back on his accumulated visits.[3] This is a system whereby an inmate can – if the necessary criteria is met – have a temporary transfer to a suitable prison nearer to their home/family. Unfortunately, like inmates often do, he had jumped the gun, thinking accumulated visits were a divine right and consequently he was entitled to them and had informed his family that he would soon be transferred to a prison near to them. The prison, it transpired, had other ideas: he did not meet the criteria and was informed that his application had on this occasion been declined. Now he was in a bit of a dilemma. Normally, when he heard something he didn't like, he'd throw a temper tantrum, smash and kick, shout at things. But that was a bit risky because it might just fuck up any future application. There could be the chance he could argue them around this time, so was it better to reluctantly accept his fate? He could tell his family the prison had fucked him over and lied to him, so that was all right.

Just at the moment that all of this was going through his head, a governor walked on to the wing. Though rare, this was almost always a negative experience as governors are in effect a massive soft touch. On this occasion, the disgruntled inmate spotted an opportunity and made an immediate beeline for him, asking why and what he could do about this knock-back. The governor, looking slightly harassed, replied that he would have to see the staff, get

---

3 An inmate high up in the so-called pecking order or the inmate's own unofficial hierarchy.

his personal officers to deal with it. The now-even-more-agitated inmate replied, 'You're the governor, you could do it,' to which the now-annoyed governor informed the inmate that he was not paid to deal with inmates' problems, he was paid to deal with problem staff!

Flip-flopping

Every single rule, every single decision came up for debate and once that process had begun, it was impossible to reverse. It used to be a rule that inmates couldn't collect meals from the servery in flip-flops and shorts. This rule had been put in place because an inmate had once seriously burnt their feet when an urn of hot gravy was upturned during a scuffle. One particular lunchtime, two inmates were informed that they would not be able to collect their meals in short skirts and flip-flops and would need to return in long trousers and shoes.

It massively kicked off, with the officer being accused of prejudice and discrimination. Other inmates got wind and joined in: 'Fucking disgraceful, screws!' We were able to keep a lid on it but the simple fact was, no one knew what the actual rules were. One rule had come in to ensure the safety of inmates but now seemed to contravene an overarching rule that protected their dignity.

The same goes for headwear. Hats aren't supposed to be worn unless it's for religious purposes but even that had become more complicated. It used to be that an inmate was asked during the induction process what religion they were and whatever that religion was at that point, that's what it remained until a formal request to 'change religions' was made. This was in place so that an inmate's diet could, if necessary, be catered for and so that any special needs were known about and factored in, in advance. The rules and regulations were foolproof, screw-proof and inmate proof, black and white, with no room for interpretation. Nowadays everything is fifty shades of grey, open to interpretation, abuse and misunderstanding – inmates and officers haven't a clue what the rules are and the rules seem to change constantly.

Governors come out of a meeting and swing the steering wheel in one direction, oblivious to the problems they cause. It's all fine and dandy for them to say an inmate can choose what name they wish to be known by, what religion they wish to practise on any given day, what gender they choose to be and what clothes they wish to wear but it causes chaos – and chaos in a prison equals trouble, something that could so easily be avoided.

Turkeys and Christmas

It was the constant need to make a prisoner's life a little more comfortable and a little less austere that saw a governor come up with the recommendation that a prisoner should be allowed to be part of the selection process for potential prison officers. Now this blew my mind. A governor at HMP Highdown in Surrey had thought it an excellent idea to appoint an inmate as part of the interviewing process for new recruits. It was deemed acceptable to have an inmate not only sit in while the potential officer was being inter-viewed but actually take part and ask the candidate probing questions. Apart from anything else, how could they not see that the process of interviewing and assessing a candi-date could throw up all sorts of personal details that could be massively useful as leverage if they were ever to get a job as an officer? Their background, personal life, sexual orientation and religious beliefs, political affiliation, hobbies, family life, previous work history, etc., it was all potentially useful. Those answers become currency, ammunition to be used and/or exploited, sold on and/or used as some sort of leverage. It immediately weakens the officer and strengthens the prisoner. In my opinion, an inmate should not know anything about a prison officer. This is what I was taught and there are many instances of an inmate using personal information about an officer as leverage to get them to 'traffic' (smuggle illicit items into the prison). An inmate should be ignorant regarding a prison officer's life outside the prison.

Thankfully, the POA got involved, stating in no uncertain terms, 'The POA are in disbelief that a Governor at an establishment in HMPPS have selected a prisoner as part of an interview board to determine the suitability of prison officers for a particular unit within that prison.'[4] The then justice secretary was asked to step in and it was confirmed that all prison governors had been instructed not to repeat this in the future. But the fact it had been considered at all suggested where the safety of officers stood in the list of priorities.

I clearly remember a couple of occasions when an inmate approached me, asking questions about me. One time I was standing on a landing on B wing when an inmate I had known for three or four years came up to me and asked me a question, which went along the lines of 'Mr B, can I ask you a question?' I replied, 'You can and if I can answer, I will.' 'Why do they call you Mr B and not Governor?' (Which is what inmates call officers.) 'I don't

---

4 The Prison Officers Association, basically the trade union for the prison service.

know,' I replied, 'but you just called me Mr B!' Another occasion was when I was at Albany, an inmate whom I had worked with for a couple of years was being trans-ferred to another prison and as he was leaving the wing, he asked me if I was straight or gay. I think he asked it in an attempt to be shocking but I simply replied that I hadn't decided yet, then asked him what he would recommend. He left the wing none the wiser and even more confused. A young officer then came up to me and asked if I minded being asked that question and I said no, I was delighted. 'Why's that?' he asked. I told him that I'd worked with that inmate every day for over two years and he actually knew fuck all about me and that's the way I like it!

It's a lovely theory, to try and break down the 'them and us' of officer and inmate. To gain mutual trust, mutual respect and relate to each other as human beings. But only one of us is allowed to leave at the end of the day. We're not the same and to pretend otherwise is, in my opinion, patronising and dangerous. If you have custodial sentences as part of your justice system, as we in this country do, then you have empowered the people at the sharp end of that system to carry them out. You can't sit in an office handing down rules that make you feel better about your role in the system, make you feel kinder, make you feel like you're treating prisoners with dignity, while you're completely oblivious to the real-world harm those policies are doing.

Assaults

Prison officers getting assaulted has always been part of the job. You're the line between some of the most violent people in the country and what they want. You can be as vigilant and careful as humanly possible but there will always be that moment someone takes advantage. But towards the end of my time in prison something fundamentally changed about the attitude towards it. We were told ad nauseam that it was part of the job to be assaulted, with one of the managers actually stating to staff just prior to them entering a cell to restrain and control an armed, very angry and very drunk inmate, that they were the 'cannon fodder'. Something has tipped in the sense that it used to be something that happened, but everything was done to avoid it, whereas now it's seen as unavoidable. My hunch is that somewhere in that magic spreadsheet, the money saved has been balanced out against the assaults against staff and been found acceptable. In my opinion, many assaults are avoidable.

In my time as an officer, like almost everyone there, I've been assaulted, punched, bitten, spat at and had fluid of various types thrown at me. I've been cut while restraining an inmate, I've had things thrown at me, I've seen fire extinguishers thrown at staff, officers knocked unconscious and stabbed. Luckily, even though officially the 'in-house' NHS Healthcare professionals are there to treat inmates, not staff, in my experience NHS staff have always come to the aid of an officer. However, how absurd is it that this is actually left up to the individual nursing staff, who are effectively breaking the rules by doing so. If you wanted to find a more efficient way of signalling to a workforce that you don't care about their welfare you'd have to work pretty hard to find a better one.

One particular assault that took place towards the end of my time in the prison service occurred on the sports field during a football match between inmates. The physical education instructor was refereeing the match when one of the inmates, who was pissed off with one of his decisions, punched him and when he went down, he kicked him so hard that he was rushed to hospital. The injuries he suffered were so serious, he was forced to leave the service. This was a serious assault but when it was handed over to the police, they were reluctant to pursue the case because it was 'not in the public interest'.

It turned out this was the third time that this inmate had assaulted a member of staff and each time it had been 'not in the public interest' to pursue it. How can this be allowed to happen? How can there not be a culture of aggressively pursuing maximum punishment for those who assault their staff in any way? There's a sign saying that in every supermarket, for God's sake! I think the reason for this is that it allows the illusion of the statistics to be maintained. The true extent of the dangerous conditions in prisons is being kept hidden by this again and again. That one inmate has three unrecorded assaults, which means he has carte blanche to proceed with his assaults; meanwhile the prison hits its targets for violent incidents against staff. And the number of physically and mentally damaged ex-staff racks up. The probation service and parole board are blissfully unaware that a particular inmate has been assaulting staff, simply because it's not in the public interest and anyway, it's part of a prison officer's job to get assaulted, isn't it?

Damned lies and statistics

It's not just assaults against officers. Drug taking, drinking, sexual assaults are all seemingly on the rise and if the official statistics are going up, in reality the figures will be many times higher. The days of the adjudication process being able to deal with broken rules are long gone. Now the system is seemingly exclusively designed to help, understand, rehabilitate, empathise, sympathise and promote as many second chances as the inmate needs. Finding inmates guilty would reflect badly on a prison and their tick boxes. In a nutshell, there really is no deterrent, so poor behaviour continues and often escalates.

If you brush everything under the carpet, at some point you're going to have to look under there and you really won't like what you find. The term 'not in the public interest' literally hides a multitude of sins, hundreds upon hundreds of nefarious activities such as assaults, drug taking, etc. that happen within prisons but no action is taken because 'it's not in the public interest'. Therefore to the 'public' everything is all fine and dandy inside the British prison system, but they fail to see that the prisoner who gets away with a particular crime inside will not be sufficiently deterred or has not learned to stop his criminal behaviour – in fact, he may well come to realise that he is untouchable.

The sad thing is that like so many things, it will be brushed under the carpet, under the same heading as the horrendously high number of physical assaults on staff, failed mandatory drug tests and staff retention to name but a few issues. Namely, it's 'not in the public interest' to proceed with a prosecution so the statistics read in favour of everything being just splendid in Her Majesty's Prison Service – smoke and mirrors at their absolute best!

A 'clearly dead' inmate

There was an article a few years back about prison officers at HMP Chelmsford trying to resuscitate a 'clearly dead inmate' before going on to say 'attempts to resuscitate a prisoner who had been clearly dead for some time have been described as disappointing and inappropriate'. The reality of this sort of thing is that any serving prison officer is obliged to protect the life of an inmate. The officers attempting to save this particular inmate were in a no-win situation. Had they decided that the inmate was dead and not tried to resuscitate him, they would have been in the shit because they are not sufficiently qualified to say one way or the other that a body that has collapsed and appears to be lifeless, is alive or dead – only a qualified medical practitioner can make that call. The staff tried to save a life and were vilified for their action. Had they not attempted to do so, they would have been placed under investigation for not at least trying, only because they were not medically qualified to say that resuscitation was not a viable option.

Brain drain

A couple of years before I retired, the prison service realised that the exodus of experienced staff was at a crisis point and that crisis point had now tipped the scales in the inmates' favour. The lack of experienced staff on the landings allowed a fertile breeding ground for violence, bullying, drug taking and any other number of nefarious activities to take hold. The decision makers, the button-pushing bean counters, would of course disagree. However, the simple fact was that after paying off so many experienced staff, the prison service eventually realised, though never admitted that it had fucked up, and decided action was needed so they implemented a huge recruitment drive. They would recruit 2,500 new officers, however their salary would be far less than the officers already in the posts and their pay, like their training, would be an inferior, rushed and watered-down affair, even though the job would be exactly the same.

Though the 2,500 places were quickly filled, they were not retained and it was reported that 33 per cent of the new staff left after less than a year in the job. These under-experienced, under-trained staff were told that the real problem in the prison service was the stubborn old officers, who were stuck in their old-fashioned ways. We were left with division and discord, constant clashes between the older generation and the new recruits. On one side, the new generation of officers believed that the old screws were dinosaurs: foul-mouthed, disrespectful and unable to think of prisoners as 'residents', they were part of the problem. Meanwhile, us older screws despaired at what had been lost. The ease with which entire ways of working were being lost, the disrespect shown to the role of prison officer and by extension, the prisoner. If you ask me, I'd much rather be in a prison where an inmate was called an 'inmate' but where some semblance of order reigned than one where an inmate was called a 'resident' but the whole place was in chaos. It's all very well to try and make prison a nicer place, it may even prove to make prison more effective in the end, but when those who are making the decisions are so insulated from their day-to-day human cost, it's the prison officers and inmates who are left to pay the bill.

One morning, just before I left the prison service, an email was sent to all staff, asking who would like to put their name down for the upcoming Remembrance Day Parade at The Cenotaph in London. The prison service is usually keenly represented by staff, resplendent in their best dress uniforms, proudly marching past the memorial and saluting the fallen. A couple of the newer officers asked if they would be able to attend and submitted their names to the already long list of officers keen to represent HM Prison Service at the parade.

When the list of names appeared, confirming those given permission to take part, the two NEPOs were over the moon and pleased as Punch, asking the old sweats what actually happened at the parade. When told that they would have to wear their No. 1 uniform, they were somewhat disappointed, explaining that they had never actually been issued with one. It was explained to them that this should have been done at the training college and the No. 1 would have been issued alongside their normal workday uniform. It transpired that the prison service had decided that, along with caps, whistles, and the boot and shoe allowance (an annual £60 payment to purchase footwear for work), the No. 1 dress uniform would no longer be issued.

The senior officer phoned the main stores to find out if this was indeed the case that new officers were no longer issued with a No. 1 uniform and the head store man confirmed it was indeed true. However, he went on to say all was not lost because if the SO sent the NEPOs down to the stores, they might be able to find a No. 1 uniform, owing to the fact that there were a few old sets of uniform that had been handed in when various officers had retired.

Armed with this information, one of the NEPOs made their way to the main stores and was directed to what appeared to be a pile of musty-smelling dirty laundry.

The store man explained that they were the uniforms of those who had died or retired and to help themselves to whatever fitted. To his credit, the NEPO's determination to attend the Remembrance Day Parade was such that he was willing to take a look. He began to work his way through the pile of yellowing, mildewed uniforms, covered in dust and smelling of cat pee. The store man helpfully explained that if he did find something that fitted, it should be as good as new after he'd taken it to the dry cleaner's. He could probably get it resized at the prison tailor shop too. However, the gap between the size and shape of a svelte officer in their early twenties and the 'fuller-figured', older, retired officer was too great. He found no suitable uniform, but came away demoralised, disappointed and left under no illusion of the value placed on respecting the traditions of the past.

Ladies and gentlemen, meet the twenty-first-century prison service.

CHAPTER 10

What Next?

I'm very aware that I might be coming over as a cantankerous, moaning old screw, complaining about the modern world. When I was new into the service there were plenty of old hands who told me that everything was, without fail, better in the old days and I took this with a pinch of salt. I'm not someone who wants to bring back slopping out and leg irons, I only ask that we think for a moment whether things that are old are automatically bad and things that are new are automatically good. Because I think we can all agree that things aren't right as they stand.

Prisons in twenty-first-century Britain are crowded, understaffed, drug- and booze-riddled, violent places where inexperienced, ill-equipped staff oversee a regime of uncertainty in which violence and criminality flourish. Low staffing levels mean at best, staff don't feel safe to challenge inmates and at worst, low wages mean they are willing to bring drugs into prison to top up their now-pathetic salaries. There aren't enough qualified staff to do the basics of moving inmates around safely, so inmates spend longer and longer banged up in their cells with all of the attendant mental health and welfare issues, including an epidemic of violence, self-harm and suicide. Medical emergencies are a daily occurrence. Staff are demotivated, depressed and often damaged.

These days, staff enter the system ill-prepared for what they will encounter, told that they must meet inmates with kindness and respect. Most of them will have left within a year. They are taught how to restrain prisoners when there is a ratio of four officers to one inmate. With the current staffing levels in most prisons, they might as well teach them how to restrain someone using unicorn horns and dragon's breath but because the pay is so bad, beggars can't be choosers. The prison service is forced to employ people demonstrably unsuitable to the role. Those who remain in the service who are qualified spend as much time making sure staff are safe as watching inmates. A policy of penny-pinching saw a whole swathe of experienced officers offered early redundancy. As a consequence, almost the entirety of the old jail craft has been lost or completely sidelined in the urgent process of modernisation. These staff then work too many overlong shifts and people are surprised when mistakes are made. It's my belief that it's only blind luck why we haven't seen an absolute disaster in one of our prisons.

Policy changes with the wind and is handed down by a succession of governors without any coherency and just to avoid criticism and save money. Why pay a higher salary and recruit more officers when you can enforce an urgent gender pronouns policy for free?

The old Victorian prisons are falling apart, bursting at the seams. Noisy and overcrowded, often missing fundamentals like observation glass. Meanwhile private prison companies promise to outsource prison while turning a profit. All this time we're sending more and more people into the system, hoping that rebranding inmates as residents will somehow magically fix things.

At the time of writing, the UK prison population was 87,900. Just before I joined in 1990 it was more like 43,000.

Before you even factor in the impact of things like spice and the huge increases in custodial sentences, you can see that just to keep the service at a standstill, we would have needed to recruit massively more prison officers over the last thirty years. Instead, we saw an enormous loss of accumulated experience. If the prison service had been in the state it is now when I joined thirty years ago, I'd have turned right around and left.

I believe to make prison work, we're going to have to go back to some of the old traditions but in a modern way. I'm sure far cleverer people than me could come up with a never-ending list of legal, moral and philosophical objections, but after thirty years as a simple prison officer, here are my simple, no doubt naive, ways the service could be improved:

1. Decide what prison is for

I'm aware that a belief in prison primarily as a place of punishment runs counter to the prevailing view that it should be a place of rehabilitation. Leaving aside whether I believe in the principle of that, it's clear those who decide such things have decided that is the case and fair play to them. However, it's beyond argument that it doesn't work. The UK has the highest per capita prison population in the Western world. Half of all prisoners released will reoffend within twelve months of leaving prison.[1] I know from personal experience countless inmates who come back to prison, who often want to come back, are

---

[1] The Ministry of Justice reported that the proven reoffending rate for the period April–June 2020 offender cohort was 29 per cent (see www.lordslibrary.parliament.uk/crime-and-rehabilitation-an-overview)

happy to be back and when released, will endeavour to come back again. The simple fact that reoffending takes place on such an epic scale should scream out to anyone that prison isn't working.

Remember, these aren't just faceless statistics. Every offence and reoffence will leave a trail of victims in its wake. Human beings whose lives are destroyed by the violence of the crime. Sometimes that can be literal violence, sometimes it can be the violence of an act that betrays the trust that allows society to function. And it's not just the direct victim of the crime but their friends and family who are impacted. Like ripples in a pond, we are all impacted by living in society that is less safe and less trustworthy.

When someone is sitting in court receiving a custodial sentence and smirks with relief, you know that something is fundamentally broken. It is my belief that there are three reasons we put someone in prison – to keep society safe from their actions, as a punishment to discourage them committing crime again, and as a place for rehabilitation to occur. At the moment, so much care and attention are paid to the final point that the other two have been pulled out of shape.

Going to prison doesn't stop you committing crimes. Some people would say that prison would stop people committing crimes if it was a more pleasant environment. And my response to that is simple. You don't remove the things that made prison safe for staff and inmates back when it was a deterrent *before* you add in all the nice things that make it an effective place for rehabilitation. If you're dealing with an angry dog, you don't remove the muzzle first and immediately let your toddler in with it.

I joined the prison service in 1992. By the time I left, it had become the *prisoners'* service. I joined as a discipline officer and left as a care assistant. The system allows the criminal to become the victim; the system actually 'cares for', listens to, helps and throws resources at, even compensates, the prisoner for being a prisoner. What we have at the moment is a Frankenstein's monster of a prison system, cobbled together, neither an effective deterrent nor an effective place for rehabilitation to occur. The worst of both worlds.

2. Make peace with impacting prisoners' rights

I keep coming back to the fundamentals. Prison, by its very definition, removes someone's rights. You're stopping them being able to go where they want, when they want; seeing their families and loved ones, having a job and spending their time as they want to. That's the whole point. Remember, they chose to come to prison and paid their entrance fee by committing a crime. To pretend that in every other regard their rights are central to the process seems to me to be illogical and insulting. In the old days, privileges were something you earned, not rights you began with and could immediately kick off if they were constrained. We need to stop pretending prison is like the outside world and the same rules apply; they fundamentally don't. We need to have the courage of our convictions and restore our prisons to a functioning, disciplined system or stop sending people there.

One of the most powerful and most destructive words an officer can use is also one of the easiest to spell and quickest to write, consisting of just two letters: NO. 'No' is the word that often causes the most problems when said to an inmate. For most of us the word 'no' is easily understood. It's simply an answer to a question and used to give a negative response. However, it seems that this word has often never been in the inmate's vocabulary and their immediate response to it is anger. Often their response is: 'What do you mean, no?' Inmates have often spent a lifetime of getting their own way and their reaction to coming up against a boundary is like a toddler: anger at the person denying them. But like a toddler, the important thing is consistency. There's no point in the rule sometimes being enforced and sometimes not. If you allow a way around that rule, then someone will find it and try and use it.

The current system is one that starts from a position of saying 'yes' to pretty much everything. The odd thing will be taken away for especially bad behaviour but in the main, everyone is pretending that everyone is a pleasant, reasonable, average human being. The old days when inmates were subject to procedures that assumed the worst and then rewarded those who earned it through consistent good behaviour are long gone. Today's prisoners are like toddlers who have been given everything they've ever wanted and now spend their time permanently throwing their toys out of the pram.

At the moment, every category of prisoner – cat As, cat Bs, cat Cs and cat Ds – are all incarcerated in what the government has deemed 'suitable' conditions. Sentences are confusing enough, so surely the first step would be to simplify them, maybe even make radical changes in the way convictions are dealt with?

The first time someone is convicted, offer them every possible resource to avoid committing further offences. Drug treatment programmes, education, counsellors, healthcare professionals, psychologists, immigration specialists, Citizens Advice, housing and employment and anything else deemed necessary to help the first-time offender avoid a second stint in prison. However, before their release, they must complete all and every part of their 'sentence plan' and understand that should they decide to reoffend, there will be consequences and those consequences will be severe.

However, the next time they are found guilty of committing a crime, they will have to do their time and serve their whole sentence in a harsher prison environment. One that has no in-cell television, no cell power. They can, if they choose, have a radio or CD player but they must be battery operated and earned, bought and paid for by themselves out of money earned while working in the prison. There would be privileges – gardens, gym, library, education, vocational training – but they'd have to be earned through hard work and consistent good behaviour. The only TV they would have access to would be a communal one and with limited terrestrial channels. Phone calls other than legal ones would be limited and must be earned by having no nickings, a tidy cell, good personal hygiene, attending work, courses, etc. In other words, a tightly regimented, slightly unpleasant experience but one where your own personal behaviour mattered. It would be explained constantly that a third trip to prison will be nowhere near as pleasant. This would be the old way of doing time with virtually no privileges. If someone does carry out a crime that gets them into prison for a third time, it is definitively a less pleasant experience. In the current system, your first couple of times inside just equip you to make the next times more pleasant. You know which religion to say you are, which gender that day, you know which buzzwords to use, which human rights to complain about, how to leverage the prison officers and the governors. Prison gets better and prison gets easier the more times you go there.

Inmates can't moan about the severity of the conditions during a third stint because it was after all they who made a conscious decision to come into prison for that third stint and they knew full well what they were letting themselves in for. This isn't some random arguable decision around rights that they're owed being taken away from them. Basically, if you don't want it or like it, don't do it! The entire system would punish repeat offending.

At the moment, a one-size-fits-all system means that the inmates who deserve it least are benefiting from the cushiest version of serving time. If you are willing to avail yourself of the help given to you the first time you enter prison, you are given access to education, legal expertise, drug and alcohol programmes and vocational courses. However, if you don't take full advantage of the first time inside or not actually grasping the seriousness of your impending predicament, your next trip inside would be much less pleasant. You can win some of those original privileges back but you've lost the benefit of the doubt. The system assumes the worst and you have to prove otherwise.

Number three onwards is unashamedly fucking awful. If you're sentenced to this sort of prison time, you should wince in the courtroom. There will be no comebacks, no whingeing, no moaning, just a deeply unpleasant sentence. If you're happy to price that into your decision to commit a crime, fair enough. But I'm with the Brazilian novelist Paulo Coelho when he says, 'A mistake repeated more than once is a decision.'

To operate prison of the sort I'm describing, you have to make peace with the fact that this will sometimes provoke violence. There will be the equivalent of tantrums as for the first time in their lives, inmates meet a situation they can't threaten, bribe or intimidate their way around. This isn't a failure in the system or the system brutalising inmates, this is the repeat offender meeting an immovable barrier for the first time. When a prison officer has the actual audacity to say no, it can sometimes be the first time that they have had someone say no. They will react in the way that so many of them have always seen people react, with verbal and physical aggression. The response to that needs to be consistent and coherent, black and white. No sneaking around the edges of it. Once you're in prison, you're an inmate, not a resident.

To staff this sort of prison, you're going to need prison officers who can deliver this hard line.

3. Attract, train and retain the right staff

When I joined the prison service, I was told the percentage of applicants that actually got the job as a prison officer was around the 10 per cent mark. These days, it's around 95 per cent, ninety-five out of a hundred people applying for this job. This is tantamount to saying anyone can do the job. Why? I'm sure that we were not of superior quality, but being a prison officer was once a reasonably well-paid, secure, long-term career. Today, the thinking seems to be that if you throw enough mud at the wall, some will stick. In this environment the fact that criminal gangs are actively recruiting people to become prison officers doesn't seem so far-fetched. Is it any wonder that when the retainment rate is so low, the prison service offers a slimmed-down training process? There's no point spending money on training officers when two-thirds of them leave. We're stuck in a vicious cycle of the wrong sort of people getting the job, being poorly trained, then being shocked by the reality of the conditions and leaving.

In my opinion it's an expensive and potentially disastrous way of recruiting. In a prison service that has made its peace with its role as the person that says no to criminals, the question then becomes, are you the sort of person equipped to say no to criminals, with all that entails?

One of the things that astounded me in my later years as an officer was the number of young officers of either gender who say they are being bullied. Now I may see things differently but for a prison officer to be the victim of bullying is on a par with a lifeguard saying they can't swim! In my rather warped world, no one should come into the job who is likely to become a victim of bullying or intimidation. The role of a prison officer, more than most other jobs I can think of, relies on an individual being able to deal with and stand up to people who are very often violent and intimidating. An officer should not be the type to be intimidated or bullied. For an officer to complain that someone is bullying them is tantamount to them saying, 'I'm not fit or able to do the job'.

I've been in sticky situations where someone has tried to intimidate me but the prison officer's *raison d'être* is to overcome and deal with such a situation. The whole prison environment is, by its very nature, one of intimidation. This needs to be made clear to those applying for the role. This isn't a negative thing – it requires strength of character, a willingness to put yourself in an extreme environment. You will be surrounded by others willing to make that sacrifice. There's a reason the prison service once modelled itself on the military. It used to be a place that tested someone in an extreme environment but that was part of what attracted a certain sort of person to it. There should be a certain hard, rugged quality to the culture. Because you need it to be able to stand up to the inmates. Pretending otherwise just leaves prison officers ill-equipped and ill-prepared and makes prison a more dangerous place.

When I first started working as a prison officer the best way to learn was by actually doing it, time and time again. A new officer would be thrown in at the deep end and given a job and was expected to get on with it. The experienced staff were always there and would guide you if you were too far off, but you learned on the job by doing the job. It was understood that it was primarily a job about people and people are always different. Nowadays, the number of experienced staff has been decimated and new staff often refuse to do whole swathes of the job. Hence they never learn. I started my career doing certain jobs because I was inexperienced and hadn't done them and finished my career doing certain jobs because I was experienced and some NEPOs didn't want to do them. You should want to gain the respect of those who are more senior to you, and you should want to earn that respect by getting stuck in.

To say you are being 'bullied' because a colleague laughed at you or played a practical joke on you should be tantamount to admitting you can't do the job. One officer made a formal complaint of bullying because an officer laughed at him for not being able to use the photocopier; another because he was asked how many prisoners were in the group and he had just moved from one area of the prison to another but he didn't know. He should have known – it's one of the most basic things, you leave with thirteen inmates so you need to arrive with thirteen, not twelve or eleven but thirteen. However, the officer made a formal complaint because he felt that because he was asked the question, it was bullying.

Prison is a place for grown-ups. At least it used to be. That was one of the things that was once so fulfilling about the job. You were part of a system that stretched back into the past, that had been stress-tested against generations of criminals; you were making society safer. If you asked a modern prison officer what they were part of, I don't think they'd know.

Prison officers are constantly being told that they have a duty of care, which by its very definition makes them carers, not discipline officers and this would seem to be confirmed by the fact that the convicted criminal is now not known as an inmate or prisoner but a 'resident', i.e. one who resides. They don't even occupy cells, they have rooms; they can change their gender, should the mood take them. Prison officers have even been instructed to knock on an inmate's room door politely before entering. Loosely translated, this means that the officer should fore-warn an inmate – sorry, 'resident' – that he is about to get caught doing something he shouldn't. However, if the officer should forget to knock and catches that inmate up to no good, the nicking would be thrown out because the officer didn't knock and had the officer knocked as he should, the inmate wouldn't have been caught getting up to no good. When prison officers are informed that they are not to say they are feeding the wing, because you feed animals, prisoners are served a meal or collect a meal, it's not feeding time, it's mealtime.

To be a prison officer in the modern system is to be constantly on the back foot, constantly apologising for the fundamentals of being a prison officer. No wonder so few want to do it. The prison service tries to pretend that being a prison officer is a job for everyone but in doing so all they've done is make it a job for no one.

And apologies to the bean counters, but you're also going to have to pay them properly.

Salary

When I retired after almost thirty years in the job, my salary was just over £29,000. The new prison officer entering the prison service today would be on £23,595. My salary was more than that some twenty years before I retired, yet the Prison Officers Association and the new officers accept this as being a fair and reasonable salary. Is it any wonder that the retention of the new prison officers is so low; not only is the salary thousands of pounds less but the pension they receive is decreased with, I understand, no final lump sum payment? It simply cannot make sense to waste good money on training officers who don't stay in the job when you could spend it on the wages that meant you attracted those who were in it for the long haul.[2] Then you might begin to build up knowledge within the prison service again.

Increased staffing levels with motivated, engaged officers who want to be there is the single biggest change to solving the problems facing the prison service.

---

2 Since my retirement, along with most recently retired colleagues, I have been sent letters from the Ministry of Justice and more than once has one of those letters been popped through my letter box, asking if I would like to return to work as a prison officer, no doubt on less money. It's frightening indeed that the prison service would like retired staff to return to the landings, the implication being that the numbers are woefully inadequate.

Drugs

Everyone talks about spice, because it's the new thing. Because it presents additional problems – most seriously, the number of times prisoners are taken to hospital because of it, which massively takes staff out of circulation. But in every way, having motivated and more fairly financially rewarded officers would help with drugs problems in prisons. First of all, increased staffing levels would stop the drugs getting in through visits. When you're short on staff, you cut corners. You have to. Secondly, it would remove the temptation for officers to bring drugs in.

In the last few years there has been a huge surge in corrupt prison staff and, in particular, prison officers. In the fourteen months up until January 2022 there were over 140 cases of officers smuggling into prison any number of illicit items, including drugs. Fortunately, however, the Ministry of Justice realised there was a problem and in April 2019 formed the Counter Corruption Unit to 'pursue those suspected of corrupt activity in prison'.

There has no doubt always been a problem with corrupt staff, though extremely rare, and certainly in the prisons that I worked in, it was almost unheard of. Nicking the odd stapler, photocopying stuff on the QT for the local golf or fishing club, nicking pens, pencils and paper . . . yes, that happened. On a couple of occasions, fiddling expenses, whether by accident or design. But in recent times there has been a massive increase in corrupt prison officers. On 12 June 2022, the *Mail on Sunday* ran an article reporting a sixfold rise in 'corrupt jailers'.

Why the 'sixfold rise'? Is it even a question that has been asked? The obvious and most immediate answer would be for financial gain. However, this 'financial gain' would only ever be short-term. Initially, big money is quite possibly paid, but that would soon decrease once the corrupt officer is in the clutches of those inmates. How many new officers think on joining the prison service that although the pay is shite, at least they can top up their pay by bringing in the odd phone, drugs or porn, etc? The prison officer's salary has been dropped time and time again – they are now paid a lot less than they used to be.[3] In 2013, the prison service saw a massive surge in officers leaving when it decided to cull as many experienced officers as possible with 'voluntary early-exit packages'. Thousands of experienced staff took the money and ran, leaving the whole of the prison service with a massive shortfall in numbers and experience. Realising that this shortfall was somewhat problematic, they then decided to have a massive recruitment drive, even offering those officers that had left – and even more bizarrely, those who had retired – the chance to rejoin the service, replacing the lost experienced officers with lesser-paid, inexperienced ones. Officers ripe for exploitation were always going to have the potential for problems. It's not rocket science: if you recruit unsuitable people on low salaries, who don't feel part of a service that matters, then inmates will find a way of exploiting them. A service staffed with people whose job it is to say no to inmates, properly paid, will be far less susceptible to corruption.

Thousands of low-paid staff working in less than ideal conditions, demotivated and barely able to articulate what

---

3   The *Guardian* reported that in the five-year period between 2013 and 2018, over 2500 prison staff were disciplined, with 567 being sacked for misconduct!

their job is and why they do it is a recipe for disaster. Rather than spend money and resources on weeding out corruption, why not spend the money on minimising the situation that produces the corruption in the first place?

You're never going to stop drugs getting on to wings, but once you're there, the one thing that is going to stop you challenging the use of drugs is a lack of staff you can trust to have your back. In a culture in which every decision by a prison officer is challengeable, in which officers are so unclear on their role and the balance of power and authority, drug use will flourish.

Welfare

Similarly, once you stop a one-size-fits-all policy offering everything to everybody, you can make sure that the inmates who deserve resources can actually get them but this should only be after the basics are covered. You should be able to move prisoners about safely with officers who haven't worked ten twelve-hour shifts in a row. You don't get good decisions from people who are exhausted. Prison is a high-pressure environment; you have to treat it with respect, and that extends to sensible staffing patterns. This is the fundamental problem with a prison service that pretends to put the prisoner at the centre of it: you can change their name to 'resident' all you want, but if you can't attract and retain the staff to cover the basics, you are effectively putting them in their cell for twenty-three hours a day.

The people making these decisions are like First World War generals sitting miles behind the front, moving their little model soldiers around on the table. People are dying but they're oblivious. But more than that, tens of thousands of lives are needlessly worse than they need to be. Those who control the budgets are mortgaging people's lives for the pretence of saving money, all while pretending to be on the side of the angels.

They've probably never set foot on a prison landing and have no idea what it's really like.

To many, what I'm suggesting will feel like a step backwards. Lord Longford was a regular visitor to Parkhurst and Albany, a slightly eccentric, controversial figure and a lifelong advocate for penal reform. He must have been well into his eighties when he made his last few visits to Parkhurst. Unfortunately, he often treated the staff as if they were waiting staff, not prison staff. On more than one occasion in the visits hall, he would wave an officer over and ask him to fetch him and the prisoner a cup of tea or coffee. He was politely reminded the prison officers were not waiting staff. Seemingly not so mentally robust as he had once been, he very often left the prison after having been reminded to hand in his locker key and visitor ID badge. To the prisoners he came across as a man with a genuine compassion, trying to make their lives better, but I thought he came across as a silly old sod with one prime minister, Harold Wilson, once stating, 'Lord Longford had the mental capacity of a twelve-year-old.'

To me there's something of the childlike view of the world that informs current prison policy. I don't think they realise they're doing any actual harm, but the end result is the prison service we see today, which I personally believe is heading for the rocks. If things continue as they are, there will be serious incidents with major loss of life. It stems from a sometimes – I'm sure genuine – desire to do what's right. What's kinder, more respectful. Thinking the best of people. Their bad decisions weren't bad decisions, they were the product of their environment, of their suffering as children, their relationships with their parents, that crime is a social disease. But my position is those are issues that the criminal justice system needs to care about *before* it sends people to prison. Once they're there, trying to pretend that prison is like everyday life and should consequently be subject to the same rules doesn't work.

We need a prison service that knows what it's for. That sets itself up to cover the basics first and makes its peace, with prison as a place with fewer rights in which those rights are given in response to certain behaviours. In the current system, the worst inmate benefits from the rights afforded to the best. In my system, behaviours have consequences at every stage. It's my belief that this is ultimately more respectful than the position that prisoners are incapable of making decisions.

At a more basic level, the inmates I encountered almost without exception respected strength and straightforwardness. There was a system and there were rules: officers and governors on one side, inmates on the other. To pretend that you're all in it together is a nonsense brought home every time a door is locked with one person on one side of it. To pretend otherwise is a patronising fantasy – the old-school officers used to know this.

And in pretending things are otherwise, we feel kinder and nicer and good about ourselves, but we cause harm. Deterrence shouldn't be a dirty word, there should be consequences. And those that work in delivering those consequences should be valued and respected for it. The opportunity for rehabilitation should be earned, only once the role of prison to keep us safer is fulfilled.

I was always taught that you should look at what people do, not what they say. Don't listen to the buzzwords and the re-namings and the shiny new policies that claim to be putting prisoners central, look at what they actually do. Look at how they treat those that deliver prison services.

I once thought that politicians were clueless incompetents. It was only when I retired that I appreciated the fact that they are in fact very clever individuals. How else or indeed where else could an employer downsize its workforce, double the workload and decrease their salary – and say, 'We are giving you more work to do, there will now only be six of you to do the job that once needed ten. Oh, and by the way, do you mind if your pension is much less than it used to be?'

They are then genuinely shocked, oh so very shocked, when the quality of service drops. They spend a couple of years announcing sweeping changes, perhaps an inquiry after things go really wrong, then move on to another department, forgetting about prison as the vast majority of the public do.

Prison is the place where we put the people we don't want to think about but they won't go away. And what they learn about society from prison is that if the greatest deterrent we have is no deterrent, then there are no rules. Crime increases. More prison. More repeat offenders. Conditions worsen. Rather than learn from this, we push forwards in the same direction, ignoring it until we can no longer do so.

I can genuinely say that the job I did when I joined was fulfilling. There was a clarity of purpose, a feeling of belonging to something. And it felt more respectful to the inmates. It treated them as adults capable of making decisions and handling consequences; it understood that prison was an unnatural state and to pretend otherwise was pointless. The deal was for the vast majority to have better lives, some had to have worse ones. To be a prison officer was to be at the sharp edge of that.

I feel sorry for those entering the job now; I couldn't even begin to say what the job is for. If I have one hope for writing this book, it's that these stories make you a bit more interested in what goes on behind the walls of our nation's prisons. Because whatever you believe about prisons and prisoners, the system we have currently isn't working.

★

I was just finishing work on this book when I received through the post a small package. It contained a long-service medal, awarded to people after completing twenty years of service. It arrived just a few weeks shy of thirty years from my joining the prison service, over nine years after it should have been awarded and two years since I had actually left.

ACKNOWLEDGEMENTS

So many people to thank.

A huge thank you to all and anyone who read the first book, *Inside Parkhurst*. It was because of you and your support that this second book was written.

Another big thank you to Robert Smith, the agent who took a massive leap of faith in taking these books on.

And to Jamie Coleman, who had the unenviable task of going through the manuscript, making suggestions and having the patience to help and advise.

To the friends and colleagues that I had the very great pleasure in working with – prison officers are without doubt the unsung heroes of the public sector (but then I would say that, wouldn't I?). I must also say thanks to the inmates, for making the job interesting, challenging and never straightforward.

And lastly my wife Marilyn for nearly forty years, who managed to somehow be behind me and push me forward, encouraging me to put pen to paper then read my scrawl.

GLOSSARY

Prison Slang and Official Terms

ACCT: Assessment, Care in Custody and Teamwork (a document that is regularly signed to say a suicidal inmate is alive)

ASO: Acting Senior Officer

Association area: a recreation area of sorts, where inmates socialise and play pool during their association time

Back cell: an isolated cell at the back of the Seg unit

Bang up: locking-up time

Block: the Seg unit

Bootneck: Royal Marine

BOV: Board of Visitors

BWVC: Body worn video camera

C&R: Control and Restraint

CC: cellular confinement

Chokey: the Seg unit

CID: Criminal Investigation Department

Claret: blood

CM: Custodial Manager

Compound: large exercise area and also a main thoroughfare for the inmates going to and from work

DST: Dedicated Search Team

ED: Evening Duty

Fab Check form: form filled out prior to a cell being occupied

Fish: tool for cutting ligatures

Flyer: go home early

HCC: Healthcare Centre

Hooch: illicitly brewed alcohol

Hotel unit: hospital officers

IEP: Incentives and Earned Privilege

Jail craft: picking up little fluctuations in behaviour, reading body language, feeling the atmosphere

Kanga/Kangaroo: screw

Kilo unit: Seg unit officers

KPIs: Key Performance Indicators

Labour movement board: board used to mark each inmate off as they went to work

LBBs: Locks, Bolts and Bars (now AFC, Accommodation Fabric Check)

Left-handed letter: letter issuing threats against prison officer

Mike unit: classes and education

MQPL reps: reps Measuring the Quality of Prisoners' Lives

MSL: Minimum Staffing Level

NEPO: New Entrant Prison Officer

Nicking: putting an inmate on report

O1: radio call sign for principal officer

Obs book: wing observation book, for recording anything of interest that has happened on the wing

Omertà: the code of silence

Ones (twos, threes, etc.): denotes the landings, with ones being ground floor, twos the first floor and so on

OS: offender supervisors

Oscars: principal officers

OSG: Operational Support Grade

Package: cat A prisoner

Pad mate: cell mate

PEIs: physical education instructors

Peter: cell

PNOMIS: Prison National Offender Management
Information System

PO: Principal Officer

POA: Prison Officers Association

Poncing: borrowing or acquiring

Potting: throwing faecal matter

PWU: Protected Witness Unit (Supergrass Unit)

SARU: Segregation and Rehabilitation Unit (formerly,
Seg unit)

Scab lifter: hospital officer (in pre-NHS days)

Screw: prison guard

Seg unit: Segregation unit

Shitting up: dirty protest

Shop instructor: oversees prisoners working

SMT: Senior Management Team

Spin: search

SSU: Special Secure Unit

Stored prop: inmate's property that is stored in the reception area of the prison

The net: radio network

Tornado: riot-trained officers

VICS reps: reps for veterans in custody support

Victors: governors

VP: Vulnerable Prisoner

Wrapped up: prison speak for physically restraining an
inmate, an officer on each arm applying wrist locks and
an officer controlling the head

Zulus: dog handlers

Uniformed staff by rank

PO: Principal Officer, the highest uniform grade (later
  CM: Custodial Manager)
SO: Senior Officer (later, OS: Offender Supervisor)
Officer: basic-grade officer
OSG: Operational Support Grade (supporting role not
  dealing directly with inmates)

AN EXPLANATION OF
PRISON CATEGORIES

In England and Wales, all prisoners are categorised based on three things:

- risk of escape
- harm to the public, if they were to escape
- how much of a pain in the arse they're going to be in prison

Category A is the category of prisoner who requires the highest security and Category D is the category of prisoner who requires the lowest security.

Male prisons are then organised into four categories too:

Category A

These are high-security prisons housing male prisoners who, if they were to escape, pose the most threat to the public, the police and/or national security.

Category B

These prisons are either local or training prisons. Local prisons house prisoners that are taken directly from court in the local area (sentenced or on remand), while training prisons hold long-term and high-security prisoners.

Category C

These prisons are training and resettlement prisons; most prisoners in the system are located in a category C. The idea is that they provide prisoners with the opportunity to develop skills so they can find work and return to the community on release.

Category D – open prisons

Open prisons have minimal security and allow eligible prisoners to spend most of their day away from the prison on licence to carry out work, education or for other resettlement purposes. Open prisons only house prisoners that have been risk-assessed and deemed suitable for open conditions.

Categories can change throughout an inmate's time in prison. They're assessed when first sentenced and also throughout their time in prison to identify whether or not they're still in the right prison category. If the prisoners' risks are assessed as sufficiently raised or lowered, prison staff can take action to transfer them to the more appropriate security prison.

If a prisoner's sentence is:

- between one and four years, they'll be assessed every six months
- more than four years, they'll be assessed every year until the last two years of their custodial sentence, when they will be assessed every six months
- in a category A prison, prison staff work with the Prison Service Head Office to check security

- in a category D prison, prisoners will not need to be recategorised unless their risks have changed

If something major happens, which changes their risks, prisoners can be recategorised at any time. Prisoners can appeal any recategorisation and then prison staff have to justify why this decision was made.

CREDITS

Seven Dials would like to thank everyone at Orion who worked on the publication of *Inside Parkhurst: The Final Stretch*.

Agent
Robert Smith

Editor
Vicky Eribo

Copy-editor
Jane Donovan

Proofreader
Ian Greensill

Editorial Management
Sarah Fortune
Tierney Witty
Jane Hughes
Charlie Panayiotou
Lucy Bilton
Claire Boyle

Audio
Paul Stark
Jake Alderson
Georgina Cutler

Contracts
Dan Herron
Ellie Bowker
Alyx Hurst

Design
Nick Shah
Steve Marking
Joanna Ridley
Helen Ewing

Finance
Nick Gibson
Jasdip Nandra
Sue Baker
Tom Costello

Inventory
Jo Jacobs
Dan Stevens

Production
Katie Horrocks

Marketing and Publicity
Ewa Pospieszynska

Sales
Jen Wilson
Victoria Laws
Esther Waters
Tolu Ayo-Ajala
Group Sales teams across
Digital, Field, International
and Non-Trade

Operations
Group Sales Operations
    team

Rights
Rebecca Folland
Tara Hiatt
Ben Fowler
Alice Cottrell
Ruth Blakemore
Ayesha Kinley
Marie Henckel